NOLO® Products & Services

⇨ Books & Software

Get in-depth information. Nolo publishes hundreds of great books and software programs for consumers and business owners. They're all available in print or as downloads at Nolo.com.

⇨ Legal Encyclopedia

Free at Nolo.com. Here are more than 1,400 free articles and answers to common questions about everyday legal issues including wills, bankruptcy, small business formation, divorce, patents, employment and much more.

⇨ Plain-English Legal Dictionary

Free at Nolo.com. Stumped by jargon? Look it up in America's most up-to-date source for definitions of legal terms.

⇨ Online Legal Documents

Create documents at your computer. Go online to make a will or living trust, form an LLC or corporation or obtain a trademark or provisional patent at Nolo.com. For simpler matters, download one of our hundreds of high-quality legal forms, including bills of sale, promissory notes, nondisclosure agreements and many more.

⇨ Lawyer Directory

Find an attorney at Nolo.com. Nolo's unique lawyer directory provides in-depth profiles of lawyers all over America. From fees and experience to legal philosophy, education and special expertise, you'll find all the information you need to pick a lawyer who's a good fit.

⇨ Free Legal Updates

Keep up to date. Check for free updates at Nolo.com. Under "Products," find this book and click "Legal Updates." You can also sign up for our free e-newsletters at Nolo.com/newsletters/index.html.

First Edition

Business Loans
from Family & Friends

How to Ask, Make It
Legal & Make It Work

By Asheesh Advani

First Edition	OCTOBER 2009
Editor	MARCIA STEWART
Cover Design	SUSAN PUTNEY
Book Design	TERRI HEARSH
CD-ROM Preparation	ELLEN BITTER
Proofreading	SUSAN CARLSON GREENE
Index	VICTORIA BAKER
Printing	DELTA PRINTING SOLUTIONS, INC.

Advani, Asheesh, 1971-
  Business loans from family & friends : how to ask, make it legal & make it work /
by Asheesh Advani. -- 1st ed.
      p. cm.
  Includes index.
  ISBN-13: 978-1-4133-1078-8 (pbk.)
  ISBN-10: 1-4133-1078-8 (pbk.)
  1. Small business--Finance. 2. Business enterprises--Finance. 3. Self-financing. 4.
Commercial loans. I. Title. II. Title: Business loans from family and friends.
  HG4027.7.A348 2009
  658.15'26--dc22

                          2009023479

Please note

We believe accurate, plain-English legal information should help you solve
many of your own legal problems. But this text is not a substitute for
personalized advice from a knowledgeable lawyer. If you want the help of a
trained professional—and we'll always point out situations in which we think
that's a good idea—consult an attorney licensed to practice in your state.

Acknowledgments

I would like to express my gratitude to Marcia Stewart, my editor at Nolo, who championed this project and led the process of creating a second edition of this book. The first edition was managed by Helen Payne Watt, whose research and writing remains an essential part of the finished product. The quality of the book is due in large part to the contributions of Helen, Marcia, and the team at Nolo, especially Ilona Bray and Stan Jacobsen.

I would also like to thank Richard Branson for supporting this project and providing the foreword for the book. Richard's personal story of building a great brand, launching a compelling set of businesses around the world, and pioneering the practice of social entrepreneurship was an inspiration for me long before he acquired my company and became my boss.

The employees who stood alongside me to build CircleLending and then Virgin Money over the years deserve a loud shout out. Without their support and hard work, we would never have been able to foster the customer evangelists and collect the customer stories which populate this book.

Finally, I would like to thank my family for their support—and particularly my wife, Helen.

About the Author

Asheesh Advani was the founder and CEO of CircleLending, a company that pioneered the business of managing person-to-person loans between relatives and friends. Subsequently, he was the founder and CEO of Virgin Money USA, the American arm of a global financial services company that is part of Richard Branson's Virgin Group. Asheesh is also a columnist for *Entrepreneur* magazine and a private equity investor.

Foreword

When I first started out in the record business, and was struggling to get by, my Aunt Joyce was kind enough to give me a small loan.

In my case, as maybe in yours, my aunt had heard through the family grapevine that I needed a loan, and when I came knocking on her front door, she was prepared with her offer. I was incredibly grateful, took it very seriously, and paid her back—with generous interest—as soon as I was able.

That loan kept the Virgin Records recording studio afloat. It gave me the time and resources I needed to make my business a success. And many years and many business ventures later, I still have her to thank.

Though my ventures and my lenders are considerably bigger now, I still witness the critical role that relatives, friends, and associates play in the founding and growth of young businesses. And it makes so much sense, really. Friendly lenders tend to be a fast, flexible, and affordable source of capital—as long as they can trust you are good for the funds.

If you can't get what you need close to home, and if banks have slammed their doors on you, get out there and keep searching. Even in recessionary times, a resourceful entrepreneur will find sources of capital from within their network or friends' networks. Be patient. Be persistent. Be resilient.

I'll say now, that when it comes to growing a business, I truly believe there are no rules to follow. What works once may never work again. You learn to walk by doing and falling over, and it's because you fall over that you learn to save yourself from falling over. Raising money to fund a growing company is the same.

This is the only book I've ever seen that rolls up its sleeves to help entrepreneurs raise business capital from people they know. And I'm delighted to have a part in it to help you get started. I truly believe that success is when you have created something you can really be proud of. So, on with it!

Richard Branson, Founder and Chairman of the Virgin Group

Table of Contents

Appendixes

Your Business Loan Companion

Some people say that it's easiest to raise business capital if you don't really need it. However, if you're like most entrepreneurs who are starting or growing a business, you really do need capital—and you're well aware of the challenges of finding it. You can't very well buy equipment or materials, hire people, pay for office space, and fund marketing without some capital.

It's just as difficult to raise $10,000 as it is to raise $1,000,000 or more if you don't have the tools to do it and a workable plan. You could be a home-based entrepreneur who needs money for marketing. Or you could be planning to build a software company. You could be raising money to start a restaurant. Or you could be transitioning from the corporate world to entrepreneurship and need capital to move from the idea stage to business formation. In all of these instances, you are likely to need funding and will need to customize your approach to asking for it.

But if you've already looked into bank loans, government loan programs, and other commercial debt, you may have found that they're not designed for start-ups with unpredictable cash flows and will end up costing you a bundle in interest and fees. And if you've approached venture capital firms, you've probably already discovered that the odds of getting these big leaguers to support a seed-stage company are worse than the odds of your becoming a professional athlete. During a recessionary credit market, raising money from institutional sources like banks and investment firms is particularly competitive, and maxing out your personal credit cards is not a sustainable option for financing a business at any time—and especially not during a credit crunch.

So, where do you go to find money that's available, flexible, and affordable? The answer is as close as your own backyard. Your relatives, friends, business associates, and other people you know (even friends of friends) are among the best sources of small business financing available. You have several options: You can raise the money you need in the form of a gift (no repayment expected), a loan (repayment expected), or an equity investment (in return for shared ownership in your business). We'll mostly leave equity investing to another book, but you should recognize it as an option so that you won't be caught off guard if you find yourself in discussion with a prospective investor (or a lender who hopes to be one down the line).

Is this book just for people with rich friends or incredibly sympathetic relatives? Not at all. As you'll read in the stories scattered throughout this book, many more entrepreneurs than you might expect started their businesses with informal loans, investments, or even gifts. These are practical, time-tested financing sources. In fact, half of the CEOs asked in the 2004 *Inc. 500* survey of the nation's fastest-growing private companies said that family was involved when they raised their start-up capital—as compared to a mere 7% who said they were funded by formal venture capital.

Millions of Americans Make Informal Investments

A total of 5% of Americans invested privately in someone else's business between 2000 and 2003. That's nearly 15 million Americans, and over half of those folks invested in the business of a relative or close friend. In dollar terms, these investments (most of which are loans) from friends, relatives, and associates add up to around $108 billion every year, or almost 1% of the nation's gross domestic product (GDP). Any way you slice it, millions of businesses benefit from informal investing. (Note: These statistics came from an annual worldwide study called the Global Entrepreneurship Monitor, found at www.gemconsortium.org, which evaluates the role of informal investments in small business financing. We'll refer to this study elsewhere in this book as the "GEM Study.")

Undeniably, there are emotional pitfalls to loans between family and friends, along with financial risks and administrative requirements. But with preparation, understanding, and a few legal forms—all of which you'll find in this book—these pitfalls can, in most cases, be successfully overcome. I've already seen it happen in hundreds of cases. In 2001, I started a business, CircleLending, Inc., that focused on just this type of financing—we managed person-to-person loans between relatives, friends, and business associates. This book is full of nuts-and-bolts information about raising money from friends and family, based on my own personal experience raising money and from observing CircleLending clients succeed. In order to start CircleLending, I personally raised several million dollars from over 75 private investors, including many relatives, friends, and business associates. Richard Branson's Virgin Group acquired a majority interest in CircleLending in 2007 and I helped launch the Virgin Money brand in the United States. Over the years, I have learned firsthand how to raise money from venture capital investors, angel investors, banks, and corporate investors—along with raising money from relatives and friends.

By now, I've got a good idea of how a wide variety of entrepreneurs can make informal financing work for them, often in advance of raising money from other sources.

By the time you've read the key information here, you will truly be ready to successfully raise funds from family and friends in a manner customized to suit your business. I'll help you execute your capital-raising objectives and show you how to:

- Do your homework before you make your first pitch for a business loan.
- Understand all the key legal and tax issues involved (from how your legal structure affects fundraising to the basics of gift taxes to what you need to attract equity investments).
- Identify the best prospects for small business loans (hint: it goes far beyond your immediate relatives).
- Plan ahead to neutralize the money impact on your personal relationship—such as investors meddling in your business or hurt feelings among relatives.
- Pull together everything you need to make a compelling case, including a loan request letter, solid backup material, and a physical representation of your product (which helps bring your business to life).

- Choose the right time and place (and approach) to request a business loan.
- Prepare a promissory note, repayment schedule, security agreement, and other legal documents for those who've said yes.
- Fulfill your obligations after the money has changed hands.
- Deal with any problems that come up along the way, such as missed payments or (worst case) your default on the loan.

Throughout the book, you'll find worksheets, sample forms, and letters, as well as references to additional resources. The forms and worksheets are both in the back of the book (Appendix B) and on the CD (what we've named the Loan Forms CD).

Money from family and friends is often the fastest and cheapest source of capital available to entrepreneurs. My goal is to make this book your companion to help you raise it and repay it successfully.

Key Features of Gifts, Loans, and Equity Investments			
	Repayment Expected?	Type of Repayment	Necessary Documentation
Gift	No	None	A letter documenting the amount of the gift and noting that the giver does not expect repayment
Loan	Yes, and normally with interest	Repayment of principal and interest at specified intervals for a set amount of time	For an unsecured loan, a promissory note For a secured loan, a promissory note, security agreement, and UCC filing
Equity Investment	Yes, but not at a set amount	An ownership interest in your company	A stock purchase agreement detailing the price of the shares, the number of shares, and the rights and responsibilities of both the business and the investor

Words You'll Need to Know

I've tried to keep the business jargon to a minimum in this book. However, for clarity's sake, I've chosen a few words to refer to some of the important people and concepts described here.

Investors. In its most technical meaning, this refers to equity investors, that is, people who buy shares in a business and thus become co-owners. However, in this book, I'll use investor more broadly to refer to anyone who makes a loan, gift, or equity investment in support of your business. My reasoning is that people who provide money—regardless of the type—to the businesses of people they know tend to think of themselves as investors. The word connotes the individual's personal as well as financial support for the business and the entrepreneur. (Nevertheless, in later chapters when we start discussing making and documenting your actual agreements with people, it will be necessary to distinguish among the three types of capital, and I'll refer separately to "borrowers," "lenders," "gift givers," and "equity investors," as separately defined below.)

Borrower. A person or organization (probably you, the entrepreneur, or your business) that receives money and promises to repay it.

Lender. A person (or organization) that loans you money expecting that you will repay it, over time, usually with interest.

Gift giver. Someone who gives you money with no legal strings attached. In fact, this category would hardly be worth discussing, if it weren't that the IRS can tax certain gifts.

Equity investor. A person or organization that buys shares in your business.

Informal loan, private loan, friends-and-family loan, interpersonal loan. All of these terms refer to a loan between private parties (such as from a relative, friend, or colleague), as opposed to a loan from a bank, a company, or another organization. Be careful not to confuse these with "personal loans," which refer to a loan (from any type of lender) to be used for a personal purpose other than a business or a home—for example, for education, for a new vehicle, to pay down debts, or for an emergency.

Why Raising Money From Family and Friends Is for You and Yours

One of the biggest myths about private lending is that entrepreneurs like yourself are essentially preying on the charitable instincts of your friends and family—using your desperation as a way to extract money, all the time knowing that your friends and family may never see that money again. The truth is much different.

Yes, there are risks involved for people who lend to a start-up business, even if those people are related to the founder. But you can take various steps to protect both the money and the relationship. And reason aside, sometimes relatives and friends are willing to lend a helping hand right when you need it most.

"The funds from friends and family was our first round of financing and let us get the first phase of our business in place; if we hadn't had that money we couldn't have gotten started," remarks one entrepreneur launching a smoothie shop in Verrado, Arizona. "We used it for the deposit on the location and a consulting service to get things going; the money played a large role getting the ball rolling and definitely was a huge part of getting us where we are now."

This chapter will take an honest detailed look at what each side has to gain from this financial relationship—starting with you, the entrepreneur, moving on to your family and friend lenders, and concluding with some thoughts on how to successfully mix money and relationships.

What's in It for You, the Entrepreneur?

Let's start with the easier question: What advantages do private loans offer you and your business, especially as compared to other financing alternatives? The four most important advantages are that private money:

- may be available when other capital is not
- is often cheaper
- offers great flexibility, and
- represents validation from your key supporters.

Private Loans May Be Available When Other Money Is Not

If you've already maxed out your personal sources of cash, but don't yet have the collateral or revenue to attract bank or professional equity financing, the advantage of private money is obvious: It's your best, and sometimes only, source of capital to start up (or expand) your business. You're not alone in this situation—many entrepreneurs face a capital gap at this most critical stage in their new ventures.

Success Story at the Good Girl Dinette

When starting her California restaurant, Diep responded to rejections by thinking outside of the bank box—and in her own backyard.

"I approached a number of banks to fund my restaurant. Each bank claimed my business plan and business track record were great and thought that I would be successful in my new restaurant. Unfortunately, I couldn't get funding, because the banks weren't giving out loans to new start-up businesses due to the increased number of defaulted loans.

"The process left me discouraged and frustrated, so I turned to my friends and colleagues for funding. It's been a Herculean effort and a great experience because these are people who know me, who have seen firsthand what I can do, and who know that I have a track record of making other people money. I couldn't have accomplished this without their help and because of them I'm already in the construction phase of my restaurant planning!"

Most banks will deem a start-up too risky for a loan, once they've compared you against the five Cs checklist (Capacity, Capital, and so on) described in Chapter 2 "How Banks Choose Whom to Lend Money To"). That takes you right back to your friends and family, to whom you are a known quantity. They know your strengths and weaknesses. They probably won't do a five Cs evaluation of your loan request or even a credit check (though you might impress some by offering to provide one). Your friends' and family members' belief in you is an intangible personal asset that you can use to your advantage—and turn into a tangible business asset.

Other options, such as professional venture capital, are likely to be a waste of your time for reasons discussed in Chapter 2. Fewer than one in 10,000 entrepreneurs open their doors for business with venture capital on hand (2006 GEM Financing Report). But that doesn't mean there's no one willing to take a gamble on you and your business idea. Start close to home and look to the people who already know and trust you, who might also be willing to put some money behind you. Chances are you'll be able to find friends and family and even a few business colleagues to take a chance and loan you money when you need it most. Later on, you can worry about attracting the attention of the heavy hitters.

Private Loans Are Often Cheaper

Even if you could get a bank loan, the high fees and interest rates might make it an overly risky choice for your fledgling business. Banks, credit card companies, or other financial institutions will charge you market-rate fees and interest and possibly high penalties if you are slow to repay. Your interest rate will be inversely linked to your credit score; in other words, the lower your credit score, the higher your interest rate. Even a small business banker or a microlender is likely to charge 10% interest or more. From their standpoint, they're gambling on an unknown quantity and want to be assured of some reward to cover their risk. These days, financial institutions are not big fans of taking risks on loans!

By contrast, family, friends, and other private lenders tend to be focused on helping you. You'll find that most of them simply hope that you will succeed and that they will get their money back. They may protest at the very idea of your paying interest, assuring you that a rate of 0% is just fine. Or you may be lucky enough to get an outright gift. In other words, friends and family are typically not out to make money off the deal. This doesn't mean you should take full advantage of their generosity—as you'll see in Chapter 6 which discusses how to pick an interest rate, there are many reasons to pay a rate closer to market rates. Nonetheless, even if you go as high as 6 to 9%, which is currently typical for private business loans, you can still come out ahead in a market where credit is hard to come by.

For example, the popular SBA 7(a) small business loan cost as much as 8% in the summer of 2009 (see "Interest Rates Under the SBA 7(a) Loan Program," in Chapter 2). If you're borrowing from a lender without the benefit of an SBA loan program (which provides a government guaranty for the loan as long as the interest rate charged is below certain limits), your rate may be even higher.

Private Loans Offer Flexibility

Loans from banks and other institutional lenders are nearly always standardized so that the lenders can manage them in a cost-effective manner. By contrast, one of the joys of private lending is its flexibility. This comes in handy at two important junctures: First, when you set up your repayment plan, and second, if and when you need to make changes to that repayment plan. You're not up against an institution that preprints thousands of standard-form loan contracts and would be horrified at your suggestion that it alter a single clause. Instead, you're borrowing from someone who is just as interested in a feasible repayment plan as you are.

When you sit down to create a schedule for your repayments, you should think first about what you can afford, and then create a schedule that makes keeping up with your payments possible. Don't assume that you have to follow the typical bank model, in which small business loans are "amortized"—meaning that repayment is scheduled to begin immediately, at a set amount for every installment. With your private loan, you have the option of designing a repayment plan that more closely matches your business's expected schedule for turning a profit. For example, your schedule could start with a six-month grace period (where you don't make any payments), then switch to interest-only payments for the next 12 months, then move to a graduated (gently increasing) payment schedule for 36 months. You'll see in Chapter 9 how to design a repayment plan to fit your situation.

Profit predictions being uncertain, however, your well-laid repayment plans may turn out to be impossible, or nearly so. This is the second time when your friends' and family members' understanding and flexibility can literally save your business, by allowing you to make adjustments to your repayment plan.

> EXAMPLE: Runako starts a catering company with a loan from his mother, set up as a month-to-month repayment plan. While Runako's food suppliers demand immediate payment, his customers are less attentive to the calendar. One month, after catering two large weddings, Runako realizes that his payment to his mother is due the next day, while the brides and grooms who owe him money have seemingly left on long honeymoons. Fortunately, with a simple call to his mother, Runako is able to delay that month's payment—without the penalties that a bank might have charged.

As long as you communicate with your lenders early and clearly, temporary adjustments to your repayment plan may allow you to recover from the many bumps that you will probably encounter on the road to success. You can call this "patient capital"—financing that is flexible and allows you to repay as you are able.

 TIP
Private loans can also help you build your credit rating. Historically, one of the downfalls of private lending has been that when borrowers did a good job making payments, only they and their lenders knew about it. Now, loan servicing companies provide borrowers with optional credit reporting services, so that repayment performance is reported directly to the national credit reporting companies. In this way, the on-time payments on your private loan from relatives or friends can help establish or improve your business's credit rating, which makes your business look like a better credit risk if and when you go to the bank for subsequent financing. For a list of loan servicing companies, see www.P2P-banking.com.

Private Loans Represent Validation From Key Supporters

The advantages of having your earliest investors include people you know may be personal as well as financial. Entrepreneurs report that the validation they feel from receiving the financial support of family and friends can be a big boost. The start-up phase is usually a very difficult time in the life of both the entrepreneur and the business. Money is tight, both personally and in the business, and even the most minor decisions count.

You may be exhausted after launching your computer consulting business, staying up late at night after coming home from your "real" job and skipping weekend social events to meet a code deadline for your first customer. Or you may be learning painful lessons about how a rainy holiday weekend can wreak havoc on your beachside bike rental shop. Your family (particularly your spouse or partner) may be feeling the stress of your single-minded focus on the new business, at the expense of personal priorities. At times like these, having people you know express their belief in you and your idea by writing a check can mean a lot.

Mom's Support Means a Lot

Russell Simmons, a leader in the music recording industry, openly admits how much it meant to him to have his mother's support when he was starting out. In *Lemonade Stories*, an award-winning film about famous entrepreneurs and their mothers (www.lemonadestories.com), he describes his early days, when he would occasionally lose money on his hip-hop events. After promoting a party in Harlem that no one attended, Russell found himself completely broke. "I remember sitting outside and my mother coming out. She gave me money ... and it was enough to start me over again and give me another opportunity. It was a tremendous push, because it wasn't the money, it was the investment in me. It was the belief in my future."

What's in It for Your Family and Friend Lenders?

The more you hear about the benefits that loans from friends and family offer you—low interest rates, the possibility of putting off repayments in a pinch, and emotional support during rough times—the worse a deal they might sound like for your lender. Yet, seen from your friends' and relatives' point of view, the reasons to do it are actually quite rational and solid. These include:

- altruism, or an unselfish concern for your welfare
- self-interest, in cases where the lender might benefit financially from the loan, and
- a recognition that by combining your resources, both you and your lender can come out ahead.

Making a Loan May Satisfy Altruistic Motives

Some people, particularly those closest to you, may be motivated to lend you money (or even give you an outright gift) out of an unselfish desire to support you. Their sense of personal commitment is so strong that it outweighs any considerations of financial gain or loss. For example, your parents are practically hardwired to want to see you succeed. It's not a far step from the pride they gain from seeing an A+ on your report card or watching you hit a home run—particularly if they can tell their friends about it.

Or perhaps you have a best friend who's always thought of you as the sibling he or she never had and who has supported you every time you've asked. That friend is likely to want to help your business for altruistic reasons. Altruistic lenders help out because they can, and in some cases, also to try to provide you a developmental opportunity and to nudge you towards independence.

EXAMPLE: When Kyle realized his own savings wouldn't be enough to launch his health consulting business, he did what most entrepreneurs do, he asked for support from family and friends. He sent an email describing his plans, and offered to send a business plan to anyone who was interested. Old friend James received one of Kyle's emails. "I took advantage of the opportunity when he offered … more so to say that I believe in him than the actual financial part of it. I came up with an amount I could do, from there Kyle suggested an interest rate and payment schedule, and I just chose one."

Ironically, entrepreneurs are often most hesitant about taking money from people to whom they feel the closest, out of concern that the lender will be disappointed if the business fails. However, it's usually only when entrepreneurs actually deceive others about their business' prospects that true disappointment sets in. No one wants to find out that their nearest and dearest has conned them. If you are doing your best at running your business, and are openly communicating about your business' financial situation, your family and friend investors are likely to be unusually patient and forgiving about the business' fits, starts, and even failure. (Indeed, their very patience can be the key to your business's eventual success.)

Making a Loan May Satisfy Self-Interested Motives

Although altruism runs deep in the human psyche, people must consider their own interests, too. In fact, experts researching intrafamily lending have found that self-interest is the main reason that most family members agree to finance a business start-up. That's good news for you: You don't have to feel like a beggar, and you don't have to limit your requests to your most saintly friends and relatives. There's a certain comfort in knowing that a lender acting out of self-interest is also a lender who has evaluated the options and believes that the opportunity you are offering is a good one.

TIP

Watch out for lenders with hidden agendas. There's a difference between self-interest and utter selfishness, and you'll need to distinguish between the two. For example, someone may be lending you money so that later he or she can call in the favor and ask you to do more than you'd ever bargained for. You'll learn more in Chapter 4 about how to sort through your circle of contacts and identify your "best bet" prospects.

Loans Can Make Money for the Lender

A private loan is, at its most basic, a financial transaction. Any lender who is not operating out of pure altruism will approach the deal with an eye toward the market. People will probably compare the terms of the loan you're offering with what they could get (or are getting) by putting the same amount of money in a savings account, CD, or other investment. If you can offer a better return with acceptable risk, lenders may well take you up on it. (Chapter 6 explains how to come up with an interest rate.)

I once made the mistake of asking a possible angel investor why he was considering my company. He contorted his face, implying it was a silly question. Obviously, his motivation was to make money. Because I had been raising money primarily from close friends, work colleagues, and relatives up to that point, I had forgotten that some of my contacts would be simply motivated by financial returns—and I realized that no one is going to protest if the loan makes them a decent return, not even your grandmother.

EXAMPLE: Sumalee wants to start a shop in Los Angeles selling Thai desserts. She approaches her tax accountant about a loan of $4,000, offering to repay the principal (original loan amount) plus 8% over the course of three years. The accountant is financially savvy enough to know that he could never earn that kind of return on a three-year CD. Of course, Sumalee's offer presents many risks—retail shops are expensive to set up and operate, and Thai desserts are not yet well known in the United States. What's more, the FDIC won't come along and bail Sumalee's lenders out if her venture fails, as they would if an FDIC-insured bank failed. Nevertheless, the accountant knows that Sumalee has a good head for business and he likes the idea of an 8% return on a short-term loan, so he lends her the $4,000. The 8% rate she offered was enough to overcome her accountant's concern about the risk normally associated with a small start-up retail shop.

Private loans are financial opportunities that your friends, your family, and even other people to whom you're not as close might evaluate and rationally choose to take advantage of. As long as you provide accurate information about your business's prospects, it's ultimately up to them to decide whether your offer has a chance of providing a greater return than other uses of their money.

Lenders Like Getting Involved With a Successful Business

Some entrepreneurs enjoy helping others get a start, by providing financial support and cheerleading in the early stages. They are likely to value your entrepreneurial spirit and feel good when they can use their knowledge and experience to foster that spirit. They did it themselves and are eager to be a part of it all over again.

EXAMPLE: Jennie is both an entrepreneur and an experienced business lender. The owner of a successful women's fitness business, Jennie currently has nine outstanding loans to friends and colleagues ranging from $8,000 to $35,000. In each case, someone she knew came to her with a business idea that was related to her area of expertise and caught her imagination. She made one loan to a feminist ethnographer, one to a water-birth center, and one to a maker of women's workout gear. Jennie made sure that all the loans were formalized with the proper documentation and serviced through a loan servicing company, so that she doesn't have to spend her valuable time watching the calendar for late payments. Although some of the borrowers are doing well and others are struggling, Jennie gets satisfaction from her involvement and support in each of the nine businesses.

Lending Often Serves a Mixture of Motives

Behavioral experts say that few lenders are motivated solely by altruism or self-interest. Most often, their decision making is driven by a combination of the two. This makes particular sense when you realize that the boundaries between altruism and self-interest aren't always clear—for example, when your grandfather glows with joy at your success, is that altruistic sentiment or self-interested pride at the accomplishments of his gene pool?

We'll leave the distinctions to the academics—your lender will probably catch onto the "win-win" aspects of your proposal pretty quickly. And nowhere is this simultaneous mix of interests clearer than in the family setting, where private loans can help maximize overall wealth and serve the elder family members' estate planning goals.

For example, in some families, loans between parents and children or other younger generations serve as a form of intergenerational wealth transfer. Parents or other relatives who were already planning to leave you money can transfer it to you now, when you really need it to launch your business, and potentially avoid taxes by doing so. (See Chapter 3 for tax implications of loaning money.)

Even if your lenders prefer not to make the transfer an outright gift, but to style it as a loan, the net result is beneficial. That's because, if you view the family as one unit, the unit as a whole comes out ahead financially: Why should you pay interest to a bank, rather than to your family (who may eventually gift or leave the money to you, anyway)? Or why should some anonymous investor reap big rewards because you had the skills and determination to make your business a roaring success, when you have friends and family able to play the same role?

> **TIP**
>
> **Early asset transfers, such as private loans, are particularly beneficial for wealthy families.** Under current federal tax laws, estates worth over $3.5 million are heavily taxed when the person dies. Reducing the estate value to less than that amount through early transfers of money is beneficial for everyone.

There's no doubt about it, raising money from people you know can feel like asking for a favor. But, if you get into this mindset, you'll compromise your very effectiveness. Think about it this way: You are offering someone the opportunity to get involved in an exciting business venture, to play a role in your success, and even to earn a little profit.

Mixing Money and Relationships Can Work

At this point, you may be thinking, "Okay, I see the benefits, but doesn't someone often get hurt when you mix money and relationships?" After all, even William Shakespeare advises us: "Neither a borrower nor a lender be; For loan oft loses both itself and friend, And borrowing dulls the edge of husbandry" (Lord Polonius in *Hamlet*). A badly handled loan or investment could probably do a lot more damage than dulling the so-called edge of husbandry. Indeed, numerous current-day commentators will tell you to steer clear of relationship loans altogether. Maybe you've seen cautionary news headlines such as these:

- "Funding and family: Mix with care."
- "It's all relative: A family loan can be a recipe for disaster … it doesn't have to be."
- "Are intrafamily loans hazardous to your financial health?"
- "Preparation vital before seeking friends and family loan."
- "Banking close to home: Starting a business with help from friends and family doesn't have to mean making enemies."

Despite all these prophecies of doom, the simple truth is that most of the relationship bruising that happens around loans occurs because the transactions were handled badly in the first place. That's where this book comes in—it will help you make the loan relationship clear and legal at the outset, to avoid miscommunications, misunderstandings, and basic mistakes. With a little planning, you can structure the deal in a way that protects relationships and allows both parties to achieve their goals.

One Loan That Actually Improved a Relationship

Jason approached his father for help in launching a business importing Shona sculptures from Africa. In the past, Jason's ever-helpful father had made several supposed "loans" to support his son's wild ideas—but ended up writing them off as gifts when the ventures fizzled.

This time, however, Jason's father had a feeling that his son was better able to take responsibility for his own business affairs. For one thing, Jason had prepared the terms of the loan in advance and shown his father a draft of the legal document representing his promise to repay his father. The pair set up a $9,000 loan.

Two years later, Jason paid back the loan in full, with interest. Better yet, he and his father both say that the loan improved their relationship. Jason had never managed to pay back any money before, in part because he hadn't taken the loans seriously. By acting in a businesslike manner, Jason was able to justify his father's faith in him.

Still, you may have more specific concerns about mixing business with friendships and other relationships. Below are some of the leading concerns I've heard from borrowers as they consider asking for private loans, combined with a preview of the best practical means to forestall these concerns. (I'll get into the practical details in later chapters.)

If you're worried that: "I don't want to disappoint my lender if I'm unable to keep up with the payments I promised."

Be sure to: Carefully watch your cash flow situation, and communicate problems to your lenders as soon as you're aware of them. Generally, when you borrow from friends and family, they aren't fixated on receiving your payments by each deadline and will be flexible if they think it will help you succeed in the long term. If you're having difficulty making payments, be up-front with your lender about your situation, and suggest an alternative repayment plan that works for both of you. In most cases, your lender will appreciate your proactive response and accommodate your request—which should ultimately allow you to get your business back on its feet.

If you're worried that: "My lender will constantly be anxious about the possibility of my business failing—and hate me forever if it does."

Be sure to: Realize that yes, lenders may worry, and business failure at this early stage is a risk you are responsible for making clear to them. If a particular lender ranks high on the worried scale, but might be more willing to make the loan with some protection against the risk, you can offer to secure the loan with collateral. Collateral significantly reduces your lender's risk because, if you default on the loan, your lender will be entitled to receive and sell the item of collateral (such as a vehicle or office equipment) in lieu of being repaid. If you do have troubles, but you are honest and open about the situation, your lenders are highly unlikely to hate you.

If you're worried that: "Even after I pay my lender back, the lender may still feel as though he or she did me a favor and that I owe something."

Be sure to: Pay your lender a fair interest rate from the get-go. Even better, pay the lender more than the money would earn in a similar investment. If yours is a three-year loan, make sure to pay more than a three-year CD would earn. When you set up the loan, point out the market factors based upon which you picked the rate. That should help satisfy lenders that you owe them nothing after the loan has been repaid. Also, by using a formal loan request to ask for the money, and then a legally binding promissory note (your promise to repay the loan) to formalize the deal, you help make clear that this is a business transaction, not a favor.

If you're worried that: "My lenders will meddle in how I run my business."

Be sure to: Formalize the loan with proper documentation, to make clear that this is indeed a loan, not a case of your leaning on the person for aid. Seeing that you are serious about treating the loan in a businesslike manner should help your lender understand that his or her role doesn't extend beyond that of a lender.

If you're worried that: "My lender will scrutinize everything I spend money on that isn't related to my business. What if I buy a new coat or take a vacation; will the person wonder whether I'm doing it with his or her money?"

Be sure to: Set up a mutually agreed-upon repayment plan, so that your lender will always know that you were current on your obligations to pay back the loan before you spent anything on yourself. Of course, if your business is hobbling along on other people's money, it's not wise financially or personally to make extravagant purchases. The best way to keep your lenders out of your business is to sign a repayment plan and stick to it.

Checking Out All Your Financing Options

f you were to ask random people on the street where they thought most small businesses got their start-up money, they'd probably answer, "From banks." They'd be wrong. Although banks might be eager to step in after your infant business has started to walk, they're likely to remain notably absent during its labor pains and birth. Most small businesses need to make creative use of personal resources, draw on their credit cards, and get financial help from friends, family, and associates in these early stages. And that's not necessarily a bad thing. This book was written to help you understand why money from people you know is the best financing option for many start-up businesses— and how to make it work for you.

UPS Began With a Loan From a Friend

In 1907, Jim Casey borrowed $100 from a friend to start a bicycle messenger business in Seattle, Washington. In 1919, the business expanded from Seattle to Oakland and changed its name to United Parcel Service. Today, UPS is the world's largest package delivery company, with over $36 billion in sales. (See www.ups.com/content/corp/about/history/1929.html.)

If you do a little digging into business history, you'll find that borrowing money from family and friends is the stuff of entrepreneurial legend. But these success stories don't mean that you should just start ringing up wealthy relatives, or hitting up neighbors at the block party, without some preparation. Whether your business is at the dream stage, at the planning stage, or actually up and running, you essentially won't know what to ask for until you take stock of all your options for financing your business start-up or expansion. This chapter provides a crash course in small business financing that will provide a strong foundation for your fundraising efforts.

> TIP
>
> **Small businesses are the backbone of the economy.** Small businesses (defined as having fewer than 500 employees) in the United States represented 99.7% of all businesses and generated nearly 80% of new jobs in the past few years. (Source: *Small Business Profiles for the States and Territories*, 2009 Edition, U.S. Small Business Administration.)

Your Choices for Small Business Financing

Money from friends, relatives, and associates is only one of many sources that entrepreneurs like you might use to launch and grow a business. Let's take a closer look at all your possible sources, to see where this particular type of financing fits in.

The first table in this section ("Primary Sources of Financing for a Growing Business") lists sources of capital—loans or equity investments (purchases of ownership shares)—generally available to businesses. The second table ("Typical Sources of Financing by Stage of Business") matches each source of capital with the stage at which it becomes a realistic option for a growing business. You won't be surprised to see that most entrepreneurs use their personal resources (such as credit cards), help from family and friends, and similar informal sources to get their business going.

The reason for this is that, put bluntly, most entrepreneurs don't have any other choice. Even if you're still wary of asking for money from people you know, they may be your most realistic option while your business is young and you have no or very few customers. Until your business begins generating significant revenue, you are only the tiniest dot on the radar screen of banks, venture capitalists, and other institutional investors. Research and common sense reveal that your best bet at this early stage is to seek the money you need from within your own resources, any business assets you've already put in place, and your circle of contacts.

Primary Sources of Financing for a Growing Business

Source of Financing	Description
Entrepreneur's personal resources	Salary from current job, savings, home equity, retirement plan, credit cards
Relatives	A gift, a loan, or an equity investment
Friends, mentors, former employers, business associates	A gift, a loan, or an equity investment
Suppliers	Extension of trade credit
Business angels	Loan or equity investment
Banks and commercial lenders	Commercial loan
Venture capital	Equity investment

Typical Sources of Financing by Stage of Business

Stage	Research	Commitment to Start Business	Product Development	Launch	Early Growth	Growth Problems/ Barriers	Midlife Growth	Maturity
Level of revenue	0	0	Under $100K	Under $100K	Under $500K	$500K–$1M	Over $1M	Over $5M
Entrepreneur's personal resources	✓	✓	✓	✓				
Relatives		✓	✓	✓				
Friends, mentors, former employers, business associates			✓	✓	✓			
Suppliers			✓	✓	✓	✓	✓	✓
Business angels			✓	✓	✓	✓		
Banks and commercial lenders			✓	✓	✓	✓	✓	✓
Venture capital			✓	✓	✓	✓	✓	✓

Minimizing the Amount You Need

Before you start planning to ask your Aunt Millie for a million dollars, think pragmatically about how much money you really need to launch your business. Experts recommend you start on a shoestring. Pouring too much money into a business at the beginning can be a mistake— and it's a mistake that many entrepreneurs make. A fair number of small businesses fail in their first year, so you're only asking for trouble if you raise and spend a lot of money, particularly for an untested business idea.

Starting on a shoestring means making the most of every dollar you have and not incurring costs that aren't absolutely necessary. For example, do you really need that corner office in the newly renovated industrial building downtown, or can you get your enterprise going from your garage? Do you have to buy a new computer, or can you use the household computer after the kids' homework is done? Can you lease, rather than buy, space and equipment? Some say that a true entrepreneur sees an opportunity where others see a resource shortage. The more you can do with less, the further you'll be able to grow your business, and the better your prospects will look when you begin seeking external money.

TIP
Starting your business on the side? Check out *Running a Side Business: How to Create a Second Income,* by Rich Stim and Lisa Guerin (Nolo) for advice on launching a new business while you're still working at another job.

Leasing rather than buying expensive equipment is one of the most cost-effective ways to avoid sinking too much money into an untested business. For example, your fine textiles business may depend on that 19th century, $45,000 loom you found; but until you're actually selling the $500 all-natural blankets it can produce, you might be better off leasing the loom (on a monthly basis) from the owner first. By lowering your monthly outlay, you also save your start-up cash for other items that you have no choice but to purchase with cash, such as printed materials and office supplies.

> **TIP**
>
> **You may need less total start-up capital than you think.** According to an *Inc. 500* analysis of America's fastest-growing companies in 2002, over 40% of the CEOs surveyed had launched their companies with less than $20,000:
> - 14% started with less than $1,000 in capital.
> - 27% started with $1,000 to $10,000 in capital.

Tapping Into Your Own Resources

You probably already have firsthand experience digging into your own pockets to get your business going. Typically, at the earliest stages, entrepreneurs rely on personal resources, including savings and credit cards, existing business assets, or personal contacts. Here are some of the places you might go for start-up money of your own.

Check All Your Pockets for Cash

To make sure you haven't forgotten any possible sources of your own money, consider these options:

- **Your salary.** Don't give up your day job! A steady income, even if you reduce from full-time to part-time as you get your business off the ground, can keep you solvent.
- **Personal savings.** You might use savings accumulated over the years, or a lump sum payment you've received, such as an inheritance or a severance package.
- **Equity in your home.** You can use the equity in your home—the difference between what the home is worth and the remainder due on the mortgage—to generate cash in a few different ways. You could refinance the home with a larger mortgage that pays off the old one and yields some extra cash for you. Or, you could get a line of credit, where the bank takes out a second mortgage on your home and gives you a checkbook allowing you to write checks up to the amount of your loan.
- **A loan from your retirement plan.** Check the terms of your plan carefully, but if loans are allowed for business purposes, this

may be a good use of your own money. Plus, you'll be paying interest back to yourself. But be careful in borrowing from an IRA; it may be treated as a withdrawal and you'll have to pay a penalty tax to the IRS if you're not yet 59½ years old. For more information, see the article "Getting Your Retirement Money Early—Without Penalty" on Nolo's website at www.nolo.com.

- **Your credit cards.** Credit cards are a convenient, short-term way to finance your business. In fact, nearly three-quarters of U.S. small business owners say they have relied on credit cards for business purposes at some point. Obviously, credit cards are a terrible long-term method, since their interest rates can exceed 20% if you take a long time to pay. Plus, these days the credit crunch has translated to lower credit limits and tougher access to these cards for business owners.

But do you have to dig into your own pockets? The short answer is "yes." No one else is going to believe in your business if you don't—and to prove your belief, you'll need to put your own "skin in the game," at least to the extent you can afford it. Some lenders may want to see you exhaust your savings account, max out your credit cards, and borrow against any home equity, 401(k), or other retirement accounts before you begin reaching for their money.

Just how deeply you dip into your personal well will be used by some private lenders as a criterion for getting involved. I've heard it referred to as a "straight-face" test: Can you honestly ask others to put their money at risk if you (and your family) have not done the same? Furthermore, lenders believe that you're less likely to walk away when the going gets rough if a sizable amount of your own money is at risk.

Of course, risking your own skin doesn't mean bleeding yourself dry. You'll need to establish a reasonable limit on the level of your personal investment and then stick to it. If you find yourself in discussion with prospective lenders who are pushing you to overextend yourself by borrowing against a retirement plan or taking a second mortgage on your home, step back and reevaluate your plans.

TIP

Look before you leap into a new home mortgage to finance your business. This is your home that you're putting on the line—don't borrow so much that your very ability to make your monthly payments is put at risk. Your payments should remain low enough that even if your business is slow to get going, you'll be able to cover them. Also remember that every new mortgage comes with fees and closing costs. Make sure these don't add up to a thousand dollars or more if your goal is to borrow only $5,000 to $10,000 for your business.

Find Cash in Existing Business Resources

You may not think you have much in the way of business resources, especially if you're operating on a shoestring out of your home, garage, or barn. But look around again at the customers, suppliers, and equipment that you've accumulated so far, and you may be pleasantly surprised. A little creativity will lead you to ways to make the most of the business resources—the assets and the relationships—that you already have in place. Here are three suggestions.

Make good use of trade credit. Find out whether you can buy the goods or services you need on credit, meaning that the supplier won't require you to pay your bill for 30 or 60 days. This gives you some time to earn the income you'll need to pay back the supplier. A supplier with whom you're on good terms may even allow you to spread your payments out across several months with no finance charges, as long as you keep up. Even if the supplier charges an interest rate, the rate may be considerably lower than you'd have to pay if you used your credit card to finance the purchase. Nearly two-thirds of U.S. small businesses reported in a recent study that they use trade credit as a form of business financing.

Explore the possibility of sale- or lease-backs. If you already own a piece of equipment or real estate, you can sell it to someone else, and then lease it back for your business use. Be cautious with these transactions, however. Make sure the fees are affordable, and look carefully at the fine print: Some overly clever buyers put in a contract clause saying that you can lose the asset if you're late on a payment.

Enter the complex world of factoring your accounts receivable. If you already have customers, you may have accounts receivable—that is, a money owed you for products or services you provided. Accounts receivable are business assets and you may be able to sell them to a factoring company. The factoring company advances you 80 to 90% of the value of your receivables and collects on them as they are paid. If you go this route, shop around for the company that will give you the best rate, and be careful of signing away additional business assets as collateral.

Ask Family and Friends for Money

Asking family and friends for money—the main topic of this book—is often the next stage in your quest for start-up capital. A gift or loan from someone you know can fill a critical gap in the growth of your business. It allows you to lean on your friends' and family's trust and support to grow your business to the point where you've amassed the revenue, assets, and credit history usually required before banks or professional investors will invest.

TIP

Did you know? Private loans are such a common source of small business financing that MBA students and finance professionals put a name to the practice. They use the phrase "the 4Fs" when referring to money put into a new business by "founders, family, friends, and foolhardy strangers."

Borrow From a Family Trust

Setting up a trust is a common estate planning practice; however trusts have limited withdrawal capabilities. One way to access this capital is to set up a loan from the trust. A disbursement structured as a loan and repaid to the trust may be feasible, depending on the type of trust, but check with your attorney to see if this option is viable for you.

Borrow From a Self-Directed IRA

Self-directed IRAs are just that: IRAs where you get to choose your own investment vehicles, rather than picking from some list prescribed by the company that holds your account. Though the IRS rules governing such loans are highly specific and must be followed precisely, in some cases siblings, aunts, and uncles can lend to your business from their self-directed IRAs. See "What to Tell Your Prospect About Self-Directed IRAs" in Chapter 8.

> **TIP**
>
> **It's never too early for a business plan.** Be sure you have a clear idea of the market and product and services you want to offer, and a good estimate of start-up income and expenses, before checking out any potential financing sources. Chapter 5 explains how a solid business plan is crucial to your fundraising efforts.

Connecting With a Bank or Other Institutional Lender

Although banks themselves can be found on virtually every street corner, bank money to launch your business can be harder to come by. Once you're up and running, bank financing is an important resource. But until your business has launched a product or service and has paying customers, your average bank or other traditional lender will probably view you as too great a risk for a commercial loan. Of course, if you're willing to put your personal credit rating at risk, you can go to a bank for a personal credit card, a personal loan, or a line of credit secured by the equity you have in your home or other collateral. Many entrepreneurs do this to get started, as described above.

If you're applying for a commercial loan with your business as the borrower, the bank will typically want to see that you've figured out how to make a profit and that you have the business assets to protect the loan. Many businesses don't reach that stage until as late as their third year of operation. When you get to this point, you're considered "bankable." It's getting to this point that can be a challenge. See "How Banks Choose Whom to Lend Money To," below, for the five hurdles institutional lenders tend to set for business loans. If you can't fly over the bars, you're out of the race, at least until your numbers improve.

Although traditional bank loans tend to be reserved for established businesses, some banks and other financial institutions do offer small business loan programs, because they can get help from the federal Small Business Administration (SBA) to lessen the risk you represent. Once you've hung out your shingle, take a trip to the bank (either the neighborhood, credit union, or the mega-variety, in person or online) and ask whether it has a small business loan program.

TIP

It's never too early to strike up a relationship with a local loan officer. A local banker will have a good sense of the financing options available to you and can help you see the larger picture when it comes to the financial structure of your business. Your banker will also probably have experience helping other entrepreneurs in your community launch businesses and can recommend resources you should take advantage of. It's in the banker's interest that you successfully get your business off the ground and grow it until you run through your sources of informal capital—at which point you will presumably return to your friendly banker for bank capital.

CAUTION

Has a bank rejected your loan application? If you're raising private money from people you know because you have, in fact, been rejected by a bank or other lender, make sure that you understand and address whatever concerns led to the refusal—before you ask anyone else for money. It's worth taking the time to fix any problems, whether the problems relate to your business plan, a poor credit history, or your personal financial situation. If you don't do this vital repair work, you may end up subjecting your friends and family to risks that professionals spotted—and you knew of but did nothing about.

How Banks Choose Whom to Lend Money To

Banks exist to make money. That means that, whatever their ads may promise, before a bank lends money, it takes steps to ensure that it will be paid back. The criteria that banks use to evaluate applications are traditionally referred to as the "five Cs" of credit. You'll want to understand these criteria for two reasons: First, to appreciate how much more flexible private lenders will probably be, and second, as preparation. By mimicking the type of application you'd prepare for a bank when approaching friend-and-family lenders, you'll enhance your appearance of professionalism and be prepared to allay their possible concerns.

- **Capacity** to repay is the most critical of the five factors. Any prospective lender, whether it's a bank or your Cousin Jane, will want to know exactly how and when you intend to repay the loan. To measure your capacity, banks will examine your business' expected cash flow, your intended schedule or timing for repayment, and your own personal trustworthiness when it comes to repaying loans. For that last piece of the analysis, the bank will look hard at your payment history on existing credit relationships—both personal and commercial.

- **Capital** is the money you have personally invested in the business. Lenders will want to know how much you stand to lose should the business fail. Prospective lenders and investors will expect you to contribute your own assets and to undertake personal financial risk before asking for outside funding. It stands to reason that if you have a significant personal investment in the business, you're more likely to do everything in your power to make the business successful.

- **Collateral** is an additional form of security you can provide the lender in case you can't repay on your own. Collateral means assets such as equipment, buildings, accounts receivable, and, in some cases, inventory that the bank can sell for cash. Most commercial lenders will require collateral on a risky start-up loan. Both business and personal assets can be used as collateral for a loan.

How Banks Choose Whom to Lend Money To (continued)

- **Conditions** refers to the use of the loan money. Lenders understandably want to know how their money will be spent. Many banks prefer to know that the money will go directly toward making more money by building assets for your business, such as working capital, new equipment, and inventory. They are not as keen on paying for salaries, market research, or your overhead costs.

- **Character** is the personal impression you make on the potential lender or investor. The lender decides subjectively whether or not you are sufficiently trustworthy to repay the loan or have sufficient business skills to generate a return on funds invested in your company. A bank will review your educational background and experience in business and in your industry. It will also judge the quality of your references and the background and experience of your employees.

Florist Uses Family Loan to Overcome Poor Credit Rating

When Jack needed funds to open his flower shop, he approached his sister for a loan. "To own my own business—a creative business—has been my dream from a fairly young age," said Jack. Unfortunately, though a master at dreaming, Jack wasn't always good at handling money. He'd racked up a history of not paying his bills on time, which had led to repossession of his car and a less-than-mediocre credit rating.

So, when Jack felt ready to raise funds for his flower business, he figured that going to a bank would involve "a lot of paperwork and possibly end in rejection."

But Jack believed that his older sister, Grace, would support his plans. To prove that he was serious about paying her back, Jack wrote up a formal loan request and proposed a repayment schedule that he knew he could meet. Grace agreed to the loan. "Where Jack is concerned, my head said, 'Uh-oh, don't do this,' but my heart said, 'He's my brother.' I ended up bridging the conflict between my heart and my mind by formalizing the loan with a promissory note," Grace says. She knows loaning her brother money is always a gamble, but she says he has a special kind of collateral. "I won't be happy if he defaults on the loan. I really don't expect it, but it's not like I will kick myself for loaning my brother money. I love him and was able to help him and it's all good karma."

The pair set up a $10,000 loan with 7.4% interest, to be repaid monthly for four years. Jack successfully repaid the entire loan. His reliable repayment record led his sister to make him a second loan a few years later, to open up a second shop in a nearby town.

Jack's Flowers is now doing well and, most important, so is Jack and Grace's relationship. Of private lending, Jack says, "I think it's a good way of borrowing money, of getting the capital you need to get past some sort of financial obstacle, without going through a bank."

Small Business Administration (SBA) Loan Programs

Most small business loan programs are associated with the Small Business Administration (SBA), the federal agency charged with supporting U.S. small businesses. The SBA encourages banks, credit unions, and nonprofit financial intermediaries around the country to lend to small businesses. The SBA sets guidelines for the loans while bank lenders and nonprofit development finance institutions actually make the loans to small businesses.

SBA 7(a) Loan Guaranty Program

One of the most popular SBA programs is the 7(a) loan. Here's how it works: You can receive up to $750,000 from your local 7(a) lender, with a partial guarantee from the SBA. The SBA doesn't actually lend you any money, but provides backup to the bank or lender who does, to reduce the amount of risk that your lender takes on. For loan amounts and interest rates, see "Interest Rates Under the SBA 7(a) Loan Program," below.

RESOURCE
For details on SBA programs, see www.sba.gov which offers a wide variety of resources, tools, and services to small businesses. The "Finance Start-Up" section under the Small Business Planner tab (see www.sba.gov/smallbusinessplanner/start/financestartup/index.html) has lots of useful information on SBA programs, such as the 7(a) loan program.

Interest Rates Under the SBA 7(a) Loan Program

The interest rate charged on a 7(a) loan is decided between the borrower and the lender but is subject to SBA maximum levels. These limits are determined by adding a set number to the prime rate (the rate at which banks lend to their most creditworthy customers). The SBA allows lenders to charge you any rate as long as it doesn't exceed the limits they set, which vary with the prime rate. Over the last ten years the prime rate has ranged from less than 4% to a high of 9.5%. You can look up the current rate by doing an Internet search on the phrase "prime rate."

To determine the maximum interest rate you could be charged for an SBA 7(a) loan, you need to know three things:

- the current prime rate
- how much money you need to borrow, and
- how long it will take you to repay it (less than or more than seven years).

The table just below shows you how much to add to the prime rate given the amount and the term of your request.

SBA 7(a) Loan Program Maximum Addition to Prime Rate

Loan Term	Loan Amount		
	<$25,000	$25,000–$50,000	>$50,000
Less than 7-year term	+4.25%	+3.25%	+2.25%
Greater than 7-year term	+4.75%	+3.75%	+2.75%

The next table uses the current prime rate to show you what July 2009 interest rates for these types of loans look like. For example, a loan for $40,000 with a term of less than seven years could have cost you as much as 6.5% in July 2009.

Maximum Interest Rate Charged If Prime Rate Is 6.25%

Loan Term	Loan Amount		
	<$25,000	$25,000–$50,000	>$50,000
Less than 7-year term	7.5%	6.5%	5.5%
Greater than 7-year term	8%	7%	6%

For information on SBA loans, see www.sba.gov/financing/index.html.

Nonprofit and Community Lenders

In most parts of the country, there are nonprofit organizations that can provide you with business capital and sometimes also free business assistance in the interest of economic development for the community. Many of these organizations serve as financial intermediaries (known as community development financial institutions (CDFIs) and micro-lenders) between the entrepreneur and government and foundation capital sources, and specialize in loans that create jobs and business ownership for disadvantaged groups and communities.

The fact that these are "do-good" nonprofits doesn't mean you should expect a handout. The interest rates they charge for a small business loan can be just as high as banks, and sometimes as high as credit card rates when they take a risk on a business that banks won't touch. However, often these loans also come with technical assistance to give you and your business the best chance of success.

In other words, these organizations provide access to capital for individuals and businesses who might not otherwise be able to get it. Many reach out to the smallest businesses, sometimes known as microenterprises, for certain groups—for example, women, veterans, and immigrants (see "Does Your Business Qualify for Microenterprise Assistance?" below). Others aim to support medium-sized firms that achieve community development goals, like job creation or minority business ownership. Many of these organizations serve a particular region (like an urban neighborhood) or a particular group (like immigrant entrepreneurs). Whatever their mission, they have a common purpose: to "level the playing field" and encourage economic growth among entrepreneurs whom traditional lenders might not consider bankable.

Does Your Business Qualify for Microenterprise Assistance?

A microenterprise is, as you might guess, a very small business. Specifically, it's a business with five or fewer employees that requires $35,000 or less in start-up capital and that lacks access to the traditional commercial banking sector. In addition, the term microenterprise tends to be used to describe businesses run by entrepreneurs who are low income or are struggling to make ends meet. There may be at least 20 million microenterprises in the United States, and possibly more. The good part about being so small is that hundreds of nonprofit organizations around the United States are eager to provide a helping hand. Many of these are the lenders for the SBA Microloan (7m) Program, a start-up loan program to which even the newest businesses can apply. Although the maximum loan under this program is $35,000, the average loan is approximately $10,000. One catch is that microloan borrowers typically have to enroll in technical assistance classes administered by the nonprofit intermediary making the loan. For some entrepreneurs, this is a great resource, providing cost-effective business training.

RESOURCE

More information on microenterprises:

- **SBA Microloan Program.** To find a microloan lender in your state, search the SBA site (www.sba.gov) for microloans. See www.sba.gov/services/financialassistance/sbaloantopics/microloans/index.html for a list of SBA microloan intermediaries.
- **MicroMentor, www.micromentor.org.** If you're just getting started, this website will help you locate a business mentor.
- **Association for Enterprise Opportunity (AEO).** This organization helps entrepreneurs connect with local microenterprise resources. See www.microenterpriseworks.org and check out "Find an AEO Member Near You" for details.

How to Check Out Social Lending Networks

Recently, more and more entrepreneurs are turning to online networks to raise business capital. Prosper.com and LendingClub.com are two online networks that enable entrepreneurs to post a request for a loan much like a classified listing. Borrowers list what they want to use the money for and undergo a credit assessment. Investors then evaluate which borrowers they want to finance. Online networks are relatively new and only a small percentage of entrepreneurs who post listings successfully get funding, usually at interest rates of 15% to 20%. However, online networks are gaining in popularity and they are part of a global trend of applying social networking to banking. Entrepreneurs should consider comparing rates available from these networks with other options.

Equity Financing and Angel Investors

You've probably heard stories from the once-promised land of professional equity investing or venture capital—million-dollar investments from high-rolling companies with endlessly deep pockets, and the like. Putting aside the hype, the basic idea is that, after an exhaustive review of your business opportunity, a venture capitalist gives you cash (usually $1 million or more) in exchange for shares in your business. (The actual price of the shares depends on how much you and the investor agree the business is worth—known as valuation—at the time the investment is made.) If all goes well, the investor eventually (usually, in three to seven years) exits the company by selling the shares to new investors, at many times the original price he or she paid you. If the ending is not so happy, venture capitalists get lower-than-expected returns (or no returns at all) and disappoint the people who invested in their venture capital firm.

The best part of equity investing from your perspective is that you get all the money up-front, you don't have any payments along the way, and your investor gets money back only if your company does so well that all the owners are grinning. Sounds like a great deal, right? Well, hold on a minute. If you're contemplating sending your business plan to a list of venture capital firms you found on the Web, you may want to save your time.

The allure of venture capital beckons to most entrepreneurs, but in fact only a small group of companies with rapid growth potential actually get funded, and fewer yet are start-up and early-stage businesses—increasingly, venture capitalists direct their investments toward established and expansion-stage companies that are already profitable.

However, this doesn't mean you should write off equity capital as a source of money to start or expand your business. Although venture capitalists are probably an unrealistic target for most start-up businesses, there are other people out there who may want to invest in, rather than lend money to, your young business. You may be lucky and have some wealthy friends, family, or colleagues who can make an equity investment in your business. Or you may find a "business angel," an affluent individual, often a successful entrepreneur, who invests in up-and-coming entrepreneurs like you.

 RESOURCE
To learn more about angel investors, visit the Angel Capital Education Foundation (www.angelcapitaleducation.org). The "For Entrepreneurs" section includes a listing of angel groups nationwide.

Should equity financing become a serious possibility for your business (or someone asks about it when you approach them for a loan), you will need a solid business plan and an experienced attorney to craft a legal agreement unique to your financing situation and help you comply with securities laws. (Securities laws regulate the offering of corporate shares and (usually) LLC membership interests.) But only do so, after you get some solid business advice and consider all the issues, including:

- whether or not you need to change your legal structure (only a corporation or an LLC can sell an ownership interest), and
- the pros and cons of sharing of management and decision making (and ultimately any profit, assuming you succeed) with an outside investor.

TIP

Even if no one in your current circle is a likely equity investor, keep this type of financing in mind. If your business does well, it may not be long before you begin generating the revenue and showing the profit potential to attract professional equity capital. If any close relatives or friends want to invest in your company, make sure they understand all the risks and don't get in over their heads. (You'll also want to make sure that they have the right temperament and experience to join your business venture.)

Advantages and Disadvantages of Loan and Equity Capital		
	Loan Capital	**Equity Capital**
Advantages	The lender has no management say or direct entitlement to profits in your business.	Investors are sometimes partners or board members and often offer valuable advice and assistance.
	Your only obligation to the lender is to repay the loan on time. Loans from close relatives can have flexible repayment terms.	You can be flexible about repayment requirements.
	Interest payments (but not principal payments) are a deductible business expense.	If your business loses money or goes broke, you probably won't have to repay your investors.
Disadvantages	You may have to make loan repayments when your need for cash is greatest, such as during your business's start-up or expansion.	Equity investors require a greater share of your profits than interest on a loan.
	You may have to assign a security interest in your property to obtain a loan, which may place your personal assets at risk.	Your investors have a legal right to be informed about all significant business events and a right to ethical management.
	Under most circumstances, you can be sued personally for any unpaid balance of the loan, even if it's unsecured.	Your investors can sue you if they feel their rights are being compromised.

How Business Advisers and Mentors Can Help With Your Financing

This book provides lots of useful advice and resources for raising money for your business. An experienced, trusted adviser can be invaluable in your fundraising efforts (among other key tasks in starting a business). Here are some ideas for finding one.

Mentors. To find a local mentor, ask for referrals from friends and colleagues, or look into mentoring programs offered by local industry groups. You can also access free business advice through the SBA's national network of Small Business Development Centers (SBDCs). For example, SBDCs commonly offer free workshops and can arrange for a business counselor to meet with you to review your business plan (more on business planning in Chapter 5). SCORE, the Service Corps of Retired Executives, is another nationally organized network that provides quality business advice to entrepreneurs. Better yet, SCORE advisers will meet with you one on one, for free. Both the SBA and SCORE have excellent websites worth a visit: www.sba.gov and www.score.org. Search for mentors or counselors, or see www.sba.gov/services/counseling/index.html for these and other resources, including special programs for women entrepreneurs.

Advisors. Some businesses choose to form an advisory board. If you decide to go this route, you'll need to clearly set your expectations of the members in advance. Otherwise, you'll find that most advisory board members expect to be little more than figureheads, lending their impressive names to your publicity materials. Rarely do such folks actually roll up their sleeves and help you figure out how to balance paying your employees and paying the rent.

Follow these priorities when looking for advisers:

- Find someone with skills, information, or contacts you'll need in the short term. You'll need help leaping the hurdles you face in the next three months before you think about the next three years.

- Find someone well known in your field who can lend you credibility when you most need it to attract customers, good employees, and investors.
- Find an adviser who is content to receive a free lunch on the day of a meeting rather than one who insists on receiving shares in the company. As your company grows and takes more of the adviser's time, you should consider instituting both cash and stock compensation schemes.

Create a Paper Trail of Your Financing Activities

Now's the time to get organized about documenting and filing the records that prove your version of where the money came from and where it has gone. Whether you receive financing in the form of a gift, loan, or an equity investment, make sure you have the proper letters and agreements for you and your lender or investor to share with the IRS.

Basic Legal and Tax Issues of Business Loans From Family and Friends

An elderly gentleman I once knew, when asked how he liked his steak, liked to answer "On the plate." You may feel similarly about your business capital—in your bank account would be just fine. But before that happens, there are a number of legal and tax issues you need to be aware of—and handle properly. This chapter provides an overview of the major ones, including:

- your basic obligations when borrowing money
- relevant tax issues involving loans, and
- the fundraising and liability implications of your choice of business structure.

TIP

Don't get bogged down in the vocabulary. The terms loan, loan capital, debt, debt capital, loan financing, and debt financing all mean just about the same thing, namely money borrowed with an expectation of repayment.

Your Obligations When Accepting a Business Loan

Chances are, most of the informal financing you arrange will come in the form of a loan. Most family members and friends want to see their money back at some point, and very few of them are ready for the gamble of equity investing. In fact, nearly half of informal investors in the United States expect repayment within two years, and only 20% of people who loan or invest money informally expect *never* to be repaid. (*Source:* 2003 GEM study.)

As you know, a loan is based on a simple idea: Someone gives you money and you promise to pay it back, usually with interest, over a set time period and in accordance with certain terms. It's so simple and familiar that you can borrow money on a handshake—but I don't recommend that approach, for reasons laid out below.

The main question for you at this point is, what tasks and obligations do you take on when you agree to a loan? This section covers your four main obligations when accepting a loan:

- documenting the transaction in writing
- paying interest to your lenders (if they ask for it)
- in some cases, setting aside collateral to help guarantee your repayment, and
- keeping up with your ongoing repayment obligations.

Later chapters, especially Chapter 9, go into all the details of handling these tasks.

RELATED TOPICS

If you're lucky enough to get a gift, see Chapter 11. It covers the basic legal and tax issues regarding gifts, including complying with IRS gift tax rules, documenting gifts with gift letters, and turning a business loan (that doesn't need to be repaid) into a gift with a loan forgiveness letter.

Loans Should Be Formalized in Writing With a Promissory Note

For your sake and the sake of your lenders, it's best to set up every loan similar to the way a bank would, with a signed agreement and a repayment schedule. Even before someone has agreed to make you a loan, you'll increase your prospective lender's confidence by explaining that you'll be following these business standards. Most of your prospects will probably be familiar with the basic principles of lending, so the more you shape your request to match something the lender recognizes, the better. Also, using a traditional banking document like a promissory note sets a formal, businesslike tone for the exchange, encouraging both parties to take the agreement seriously.

After the loan has been made, the fact that you put your agreement into writing actually increases the chances that you'll successfully repay it and thus protect your relationship with your lender. The written

Saved by Promissory Notes: Renaldo's Restaurant

After two years in the restaurant business, Renaldo felt that success was on the way, but he still wasn't making enough money for a bank to take his loan request seriously. Yet Renaldo needed a significant sum in order to purchase new refrigeration equipment. Fortunately, Renaldo had the respect of his colleagues in the food industry, two of whom independently decided to lend him the needed money. At different times, over a beer at Renaldo's bar, each agreed to a three-year loan—and sealed the deal with nothing more than a handshake.

Renaldo had every intention of repaying his lenders and assumed he would pay each in one lump sum at the end of the three years. His colleagues, however, assumed differently. One expected regular monthly payments; the other expected monthly interest-only payments with a lump sum payment at the end. Sure enough, the conflicting assumptions quickly rose to the fore. Thrust into financially insecure positions, the lenders started mistrusting Renaldo, who became distressed at the deterioration of his relationships and the looming, unanticipated monthly payment obligations.

Renaldo finally realized he needed to formalize each loan. Through brief phone calls, he clarified what each lender expected and drafted two promissory notes. He created custom payment schedules that were appropriate to each of his two lender's wishes, but also long enough that he would be able to afford the regular payments. Renaldo thus saved both his relationships and his affordable and flexible sources of business capital.

documents will spell out in detail when and how you're expected to repay—including what to do if you realize you're going to be late. Once your business gets underway, you'll have plenty of other issues to think about, and trying to remember what you and your lender informally agreed to over lunch should not be one of them.

The name of the legal document that a bank would use to formalize a loan, and that you should use, too, is a "promissory note." This is a piece of paper that says, in effect, "In return for giving me $X, I promise to pay you $Y plus interest of Z%." Once you've signed the promissory note, it's legally binding. That doesn't, however, mean that preparing one requires a team of lawyers or pages of fine print. Your promissory note can be as brief as one page, as long as it covers the material detailed in Chapter 9, such as the interest rate and repayment schedule.

Most Loans Require You to Pay Interest

When you borrow, you're using the lender's money—money that this person could be using elsewhere—and in most cases, you'll need to pay for the privilege. If you've ever taken out a car or home loan, you're probably used to the way an interest rate is set, as a fixed or variable percentage of the total amount of the loan. Monthly payments are ordinarily calculated to include a portion of the loan, called the "principal," plus interest.

Friends and family who lend you money are often willing to do so at below-market interest rates. Chances are they're more interested in supporting your efforts than in turning a profit, and some might even insist on earning no interest at all.

As you prepare to approach prospective lenders, however, you should plan on paying interest, for several reasons. Most important, you need to ensure that you meet IRS guidelines for private lending (more on this below). Also, just because Aunt Jean adores you doesn't mean she doesn't deserve to earn interest on her loan. A respectable interest rate, something like what she'd earn on a savings account or CD, may make her feel happier about the whole arrangement. And for prospective lenders who aren't that close to you, offering an interest rate that exceeds what they'd earn elsewhere is a great way to attract their attention.

RELATED TOPICS

Choosing the right interest rate and repayment schedule are important parts of preparing your loan request. You'll learn more about how to choose the right rate and schedule in Chapter 6.

You May Also Need to Offer Collateral

When banks decide whether to make loans, especially to new businesses, they carefully scrutinize the creditworthiness of the borrower. But even that isn't usually enough for them. To make doubly sure that you will actually pay them back, banks often insist that you "secure" their loan by naming a piece of property that they can sell if you don't make your loan payments. This property is known as "collateral" or "security." Your promise of the collateral must be recorded both in the promissory note and in a security agreement.

The most familiar example of a secured loan is a home mortgage, in which the home itself serves as security, which the bank can sell, or "foreclose" on, if you fail to make the mortgage payments. Business loans tend to be secured by business assets, such as machinery or real estate, or the owner's personal assets, such as your home or car. It's unlikely that the people with whom you're close will ask you to provide collateral for your loan. Unlike bank loans, most private loans, especially between relatives, are "unsecured." Private lenders usually like to have a promissory note, but no more. For most of them, your word is good enough when it comes to your intention of making good on the promissory note.

CAUTION

Just because a loan is unsecured doesn't mean that the lender has no recourse if you fail to repay it. Your lender is legally entitled to sue you for repayment, which may ultimately give the lender access to some of your assets.

Regardless of whether your friends and family lenders are likely to insist on it, there may be a good reason to offer some of them a secured loan (and I explain how in Chapter 9). Telling someone that you are willing to put your home or equipment on the line says a lot. Also, it may be a key protection for lenders who later need that money for some other purpose, such as retirement or their children's education. Just don't forget that you risk losing the asset—such as an important piece of business equipment or your home—if you can't pay back the loan.

Loans Require Ongoing Management

Assuming you negotiate a traditional loan arrangement, you'll probably have to make monthly payments to your lender, by a certain date each month. If you're the sort who sometimes forgets to pay the credit card bill on time, you may find that this requires developing new habits and organizational skills.

In addition, committing to a loan repayment plan assumes that your business really will make money—which no one can guarantee. At least you'll have the advantage of working with a private lender, who is likely to be flexible when you can't meet your repayment obligations—but you nevertheless need to seriously consider whether you and your business can handle these monthly payments before signing onto a loan.

The Limited Began With a Loan From the Founder's Aunt

Know the trendy clothing store called The Limited? In 1963, after a disagreement with his Russian immigrant father about how to run the family clothing shop, Leslie Wexner borrowed $5,000 from his aunt to open a small women's retail shop called Leslie's Limited. The Limited now operates around 5,600 U.S. stores and earns $10.1 billion in annual revenues. (See Wexner's biography at http://en.wikipedia.org.)

Tax Implications of Your Choice of Capital

No introduction to getting business financing from private individuals would be complete without a discussion of tax implications. Transactions within a family group are especially likely to come under special IRS scrutiny. The IRS simply presumes that any transfer between family members is a gift, unless it sees proof to the contrary.

You'll see in this section how the IRS views loans related to business financing. Your goal should be to minimize your tax liability, as well as the liability of your lender or investor.

When Loans May Lead to Tax Liability

Your private loan is not as private as you might think. For one thing, if the IRS sees the funds in your bank account and you can't prove they're from a loan, the IRS may treat the transfer as a gift. For another, if you don't pay interest at the minimum IRS-recommended rate, the IRS may assume your lender had, in fact, received the extra interest and then gifted it back to you.

Tax Liability for Disguised Gifts

If you don't create documents showing that this money transfer was a loan, the folks at the IRS might suspect that it was actually a gift covered by IRS gift tax rules (a subject covered in Chapter 11). The IRS pays particular attention to intrafamily loans and assumes that there may be a gift hidden in them that should be taxed (as discussed in the following section, this issue affects the lender's taxes). Especially if you're planning to borrow from a relative, the most effective way to protect everyone involved is to use a detailed promissory note (such as the one in this book) specifying your intent to repay the money, the time frame in which the loan will be repaid, and the amount of interest charged.

If the loan is very large and you want to be extra safe, some attorneys recommend that you also create proof that repayments are being made, such as a loan log or bank records of deposited checks. That will create a paper trail in case the IRS comes sniffing around. Be cautious: Your lenders will not want to have their "loan" assessed as a "gift," especially if it causes them to exceed the gifting limit. If you have any concerns (for example, if your lender gives you periodic "gifts" of your repayments), consult with your accountant or a tax attorney.

> (!) CAUTION
> **If you are borrowing a large amount of money for an extended period of time,** be sure you consult with an experienced attorney about gift and tax issues, including how any outstanding loans will be treated should the lender die before you repay the debt.

Tax Liability If You Pay Too Little Interest

In the IRS's unending search for taxable income, it keeps an eye out for cases where lenders receive less interest than they should. As for how low the IRS thinks an interest rate should go, it publishes this information monthly, as the so-called Applicable Federal Rate (AFR). If you pay less than the AFR on a private loan of more than $10,000 (there is no such requirement for loans of less than $10,000), the IRS will apply the AFR and calculate what you should have been paying. This is called "imputing interest."

The IRS will then treat the difference between what your lender actually received from you and what he or she should have received (namely, the AFR) as a gift. If that makes the gifts from your lender to you exceed $13,000 (the IRS annual limit on gifts), then your lender will have to file a gift tax return for the amount over $13,000.

Although filing the return is a pain, the lender's overall gift tax liability may not actually increase by much. You'd need to have a huge loan for the imputed interest in one year to exceed $13,000. (For example, if you're paying 1% on a loan on which the IRS says you should be paying 4%, the loan would have to be $3.3 million before the imputed interest exceeded the $13,000 annual gift exclusion!)

The upshot is that, for any loan over $10,000, the IRS will be expecting the borrower to pay at least the AFR. If you pay less than that, you can assume that the IRS will start imputing interest and will keep tabs on the amount as it relates to the lender's total gift tax liability.

TIP
Don't feel bound to the AFR. If you think your lender is willing to charge you a very low interest rate, don't be afraid to save money by selecting an interest rate below the AFR. Even if your lender charges you 1%, chances are the amount of interest the IRS imputes will not exceed the $13,000 gift exclusion for each year.

Below is a sample AFR table, from September 2009. These numbers change monthly (but not drastically), so when you're ready to sign a promissory note, check the latest AFR on the IRS website. Go to www.irs.gov and search for "AFR." The first document that comes up should be the "Index of Applicable Federal Rates." Click that link and you'll be taken to a list, arranged in date order; download the most recent table.

To use the AFR table, match the term of your loan with the frequency of payments that you promise to make. For example, using the table below, a four-year loan to be repaid monthly should be paying at least 2.83% in interest.

Sample AFR Table				
September 2009	**Period for Compounding**			
Loan Term	**Annually**	**Semiannually**	**Quarterly**	**Monthly**
Short Term (<3 yrs)	.84%	.84%	.84%	.84%
Mid Term (3-9 yrs)	2.87%	2.85%	2.84%	2.83%
Long Term (>9 yrs)	4.38%	4.33%	4.31%	4.29%

When Loans May Lead to Tax Deductions

There are a few benefits to the IRS learning about your loan: You may be able to deduct your loan setup costs as well as your interest payments. As you probably know, deductions are subtracted from your taxable income, thereby indirectly reducing your overall tax bill. Also, if all else fails and you default on the loan, your lender might be able to claim a tax deduction (as covered in the Chapter 10 discussion of loan defaults).

Tax Deductions Based on Setup and Interest Costs

The two most relevant tax deductions for a new small business owner based on your loan are:

- the costs of setting up the loan, and
- your interest payments.

You are allowed to deduct (as a business expense) business start-up costs, up to a maximum dollar amount set by the IRS in the year the business is launched. For the 2009 tax year that figure was $5,000. The costs of setting up and managing your private loan—for example, photocopying your loan proposal, paying for your lender's lunch, hiring an accountant or attorney to help, and the like—are all deductible under this provision. Second, you can deduct as a business expense all interest that you pay or accrue during the tax year on debts related to your business, so long as all of the following are true:

- You are legally liable for the debt.
- Both you and the lender intend that the debt be repaid.
- You and the lender have a true debtor-creditor relationship.

Formalizing your private loan with a promissory note (which you'll learn to create in Chapter 9) will help you meet these requirements.

 **RESOURCE**

Where to find details on the tax implications of borrowing business capital. To learn more about deductions for your private loan, see IRS Publication 535, *Business Expenses.* For more tips on tax deductions from which you might benefit, see "Small Business Tax FAQ" and related articles on Nolo's website at www.nolo.com, as well as *Deduct It! Lower Your Small Business Taxes,* by Stephen Fishman (Nolo).

Bad-Debt Tax Deductions for Your Lender

If your worst-case scenario occurs and you default on your loan, your lender will probably want to claim a bad-debt deduction. The least you can do is to help the person claim this deduction successfully. As mentioned earlier, the IRS assumes that intrafamily transfers of money are gifts, so if your lender tries to claim a bad-debt deduction when you can't repay, expect the IRS to scrutinize the whole affair.

One attorney describes a situation where a mother wrote her son a check for over $100,000 towards his farming operation. Their agreement was informal. For the first few years, the operation did well and the son made regular payments to the mother. But then came a drought, and before long, not only had the son's payments dried up, but the mother ended up having to pay off a bank loan her son had taken out while trying to keep the ill-fated operation afloat. That tax year she took a tax deduction of nearly the whole amount, but the IRS rebuffed her, saying that no evidence existed to show that she'd expected repayment from her son. She appealed to a judge, but he agreed with the IRS, noting that neither mother nor son had treated the transaction as an enforceable loan. (Find this and other real-life stories at www.taxfables.com.)

To avoid a situation ending like this, your lender must prove two things: that he or she indeed loaned you the money, and that he or she took the necessary steps to try and collect upon the loan. Here's what you can do to help your lender make the case for a bad-debt deduction (hopefully, this won't become an issue, but better to be prepared):

- **Make sure your lender has a copy of the promissory note.** If, for some reason, your lender has lost the original, make him or her a copy of yours. (If you have to go through a default, you and your lender will both be relieved that you properly formalized the loan with a promissory note.)
- **Provide dated copies of evidence that the lender tried to get the money back from you.** Reminder emails and letters, for example,

are good forms of evidence (hopefully, you'll have kept them all carefully filed away). If you're using a third party to service your loan, this company or professional should be able to provide these records for you. The IRS will expect to see that your lender behaved like any normal lender would when you refused to pay and wrote you serious letters or hired a collection agency to attempt to recover the funds.

- **Write a letter to your lender.** The letter should acknowledge that the lender made many attempts to collect upon the loan and that you are unable to pay. Provide a personal financial statement, if possible, showing that you are unable to pay.

How Your Business' Legal Structure Can Affect Your Fundraising Efforts

If you're still deciding on a legal structure for your business—that is, choosing whether to operate as a sole proprietorship, partnership, corporation, or an LLC—you're probably weighing the advantages and disadvantages when it comes to ease of setup, degree of personal liability, tax advantages, and the like. Let me, however, add one more consideration to the mix: your fundraising possibilities.

An entrepreneur running a solo, unincorporated Web design shop from home will have different fundraising options than those of the founders of an incorporated Web design company. The solo entrepreneur can't, for example, raise equity capital, because selling equity shares means dividing up ownership, and it's impossible to have more than one owner in a so-called "sole" proprietorship.

Even a solo entrepreneur who brings in a second person and starts a partnership will have trouble raising equity capital, because as co-owners, the investors will be just as liable for the company's debts and liabilities as the owner will. These limitations on fundraising by sole proprietorships and partnerships are perhaps the most important issues to understand, but there are other layers to the analysis, as covered below.

Picking the right legal structure can be a complicated decision, because you need to be able to look into your crystal ball and project how big you want to get and what type of capital you'll need in order to get there. The sections below give you a primer on balancing fundraising and other considerations, such as personal liability protection. Also, see "Ways to Organize Your Business," below, for a summary of the key advantages and drawbacks to these five legal structures.

> TIP
> **Your legal structure is not set in stone.** Make the most informed choice possible now, to save on setup costs and paperwork. But, remember that you can always change the legal structure later, to fit the needs of your growing business—for example, if you want to take in investors or need to limit your personal liability because you've expanded your online crafts business to a retail store.

Sole Proprietorship

Most small businesses are organized as sole proprietorships, at least at the beginning. This is, by far, the cheapest and easiest way to set up a business—with a single owner, who receives and reports all the profits and is responsible for any debts or liabilities. Establishing a sole proprietorship requires almost no formalities, and you'll personally own your business assets.

The main drawback to sole proprietorships is that personal liability means personal risk—you could literally lose your shirt because of unexpected business losses or lawsuits that are not covered by your insurance.

Finally, since a sole proprietorship can have, by definition, only one owner, you will not be able to raise capital by selling shares in your business, unless you change to a legal structure that can accommodate multiple owners, such as a corporation or an LLC.

EXAMPLE: Jamie, who has always loved kayaking, starts a small one-person business renting three kayaks for either personal use or guided tours. After a glowing write-up in a popular sporting magazine, he is flooded with customers. Jamie decides to raise capital to grow Jamie's Kayaks into Jamie's Outdoor Play, a year-round multisport expedition and outdoor gear company.

Jamie's first loan, of $10,000, is from his friend Josh, a fellow boating enthusiast. Jamie knows that, as the sole owner, he will be personally liable for that loan. Jamie next approaches his father-in-law—who is interested in the business but turns out to be a business angel who would rather make a $50,000 investment and become a co-owner. If Jamie wants this investment, he will need to change the legal structure to one that offers his father-in-law both a share of the company in exchange for his investment and protection from the company's liabilities (a protection nearly all investors expect).

Partnership

A partnership is a relatively simple and inexpensive way to organize a business that has more than one owner. In a general partnership, you and your partners jointly own your business's assets and liabilities, usually based on how much each partner brings to the table. Small groups of people who want to pool some resources for a business or real estate project tend to use the partnership structure to do it. Again, however, personal liability is an issue—both you and your partners will be personally liable for the debts of the partnership.

One way to get around the liability problem of a general partnership is to invite certain partners—in particular, any investors—to join as "limited partners." As long as these new partners remain "passive investors," meaning they take no role in running the business, they are protected by "limited personal liability." That means they are liable only up to the amount that they contributed to the business. Another advantage to limited partnerships is that they allow you to invite investors in without dealing with the complexities of selling ownership shares and managing equity investors. (Limited partnerships are most often used in real estate, so that one or more general partners can buy and sell properties while the limited partners provide the capital.)

Jamie, in the kayak example above, could invite his father-in-law to invest as a limited partner. If his father-in-law agreed to this, he'd have the semi-comfort of knowing that as a limited partner he is liable only to the extent of the investment he made in the business, and not for any business debts or liabilities that arise out of the negligence of Jamie or another partner or manager. For example, if a customer drowned on a business-led outing and the customer's family sued the business for $5 million, a limited partner would not be liable.

However, if Jamie achieves the growth he projects in his business plan, Jamie's Outdoor Play will be on track to being a very profitable business, and his father-in-law might prefer to have an actual ownership stake through a corporate or an LLC structure. As a limited partner in the growing business, Jamie's father-in-law would be entitled only to those profits that are passed through to the limited partners as designated by the partnership agreement.

> **TIP**
>
> **Plan on repaying your debts, no matter what business structure you choose.** I'm not counseling you to find a structure that allows you to wriggle out of your obligations. I assume that your intentions are to make responsible use of your family's and friends' money—and that you'll try to repay them regardless of whether your corporate structure allows otherwise.

C Corporation

If you set up your business as a C corporation (the standard, most-commonly used corporate structure), it becomes its own legal entity. The corporation, not its owners, will own your business' assets and liabilities. This ingenious structure acts as a buffer, since neither you nor your investors are personally liable for unpaid debts of the business. In fact, if you plan on selling any shares in your business to investors (in the form of stock), or if you dream of one day "going public," forming a corporation (or an LLC, as described in the next section) is an obvious choice for you.

If, in the earlier example, Jamie's friend Josh had made his $10,000 loan to "Jamie's Outdoor Play, Inc.," rather than to Jamie himself, he'd have to sue the corporate entity if Jamie failed to repay—and would have no recourse against Jamie himself (unless he had gotten Jamie to personally guarantee the loan, which many lenders understandably do). See "Is It a Personal Loan or a Business Loan?" below, for more on this subject. If Jamie's corporation went bankrupt before repaying, Josh, as a lender, would be among the first in line for repayment—but he would have to hope that the company had enough assets to repay him, because he couldn't get the money directly from Jamie (again, unless he'd had Jamie personally guarantee the loan).

During your efforts to raise loan capital, you may well find that, especially in the early days, lenders want reassurance that someone will be responsible for the corporation's debts. That someone will most likely be you. You may well be asked to personally guarantee loans, meaning you pledge your personal assets as a backup if the business' assets are insufficient to pay off the debt. In fact, the SBA requires that all owners with more than 20% equity in a business provide a personal guaranty before they receive an SBA-backed loan, so that if the business fails, the lender has recourse against you personally. Still, this doesn't cancel out the benefits of incorporating—it's the unexpected liabilities you should be most worried about.

S Corporation

More and more entrepreneurs are taking advantage of an IRS tax status for corporations called "Subchapter S tax status." While regular C corporations pay corporate federal income tax, an S corporation does not. Instead, the S corporation's tax obligations are passed through to, and paid by, its owners, on their personal tax returns. This avoids the problem of "double taxation," the bane of investors in C corporations.

It's called double taxation because the C corporation must pay taxes on any profits it makes before it distributes profits to shareholders, yet the shareholders must also pay taxes after they receive these distributions (in the form of dividends or other gains). The net result to shareholders in a C corporation is that there's less money to be shared after the IRS has taken its cut, making an S corporation structure tempting to potential investors.

Also, even if your S corporation loses money, there's some good news for your equity investors (if any). An S corporation passes both gains *and* losses through to its shareholders, who must then report both on their personal income taxes. They can use these pass-through losses to offset their other sources of personal income, potentially lowering their overall tax bill.

Before you leap at S corporation status, however, realize that it's really designed for smaller companies sharing ownership between the founder and a few investors. In fact, to be eligible for Subchapter S tax status, your corporation must have 75 or fewer stockholders, all of whom are resident aliens or citizens, and you must issue only one class of stock. In addition, no other corporations may be investors in your company, only individuals.

Limited Liability Company (LLC)

The LLC structure is an increasingly popular legal structure for growing small businesses. It is distinct from any of the three structures listed previously, yet offers a combination of their advantages. Structuring your business as an LLC offers you (and any equity investors) both the limited personal liability of a corporation and the pass-through tax advantages of a partnership or an S corporation. For example, LLCs usually have a clause in their operating agreement detailing the formula used to determine the annual profits each member will receive. The most common formula is the member's share of profits times his or her tax rate.

Even better, LLCs are fairly simple to set up. Given the choice between an LLC and a corporation, experts agree that most small business owners would be better off forming an LLC.

Is It a Personal Loan or a Business Loan?

People in the early stages of raising money for their business often have questions about the difference between a personal loan and a business loan. Here are the basics: In a personal loan, you sign the promissory note in your own name, so you, as the individual, are the borrower. In a business loan, you sign it as an agent of the business, so the business entity is the borrower. This is an important distinction because you're not legally entitled to deduct certain business expenses on a personal loan.

Once you understand what type of entity you want to be, register with your secretary of state's office (to find yours, see the website of the National Association of Secretaries of State (NASS) at www.nass.org). You then can borrow in the business' name, structure a true business loan, and legally deduct setup fees and interest paid as a business expense.

The Chapter 9 discussion of promissory notes includes instructions on how to sign as an individual or business.

RESOURCE

Want more detailed information on choosing or changing your legal structure? Nolo's website (www.nolo.com) includes hundreds of free articles on small business issues. Search "Starting a Business" for whatever topic interests you. Nolo also publishes several books that are especially useful for start-ups, including:

- *The Small Business Start-Up Kit: A Step-by-Step Legal Guide,* by Peri Pakroo, discusses each of the five entity options described above, and includes material that is relevant in all 50 states, as well as advice on writing a business plan, drafting contracts, and managing finances.
- *LLC or Corporation? How to Choose the Right Form for Your Business,* by Anthony Mancuso, will help you determine which legal structure is best for your business, and how to convert from one business entity to another.

- *Form Your Own Limited Liability Company,* by Anthony Mancuso, provides forms, step-by-step instructions, and guidance on forming an LLC in all 50 states.
- *Tax Savvy for Small Business,* by Frederick W. Daily, covers the ins and outs of the tax code for small businesses and tax issues relevant to each type of legal structure.

Ways to Organize Your Business		
Type of Entity	Main Advantages	Main Drawbacks
Sole Proprietorship	Simple and inexpensive to create and operate Owner reports profit or loss on his or her personal tax return	Owner personally liable for business debts
General Partnership	Simple and inexpensive to create and operate Owners (partners) report their share of profit or loss on their personal tax returns	Owners (partners) personally liable for business debts
Limited Partnership	Limited partners have limited personal liability for business debts as long as they don't participate in management General partners can raise cash without involving outside investors in management of business	General partners personally liable for business debts More expensive to create than general partnership Suitable mainly for companies that invest in real estate
Regular Corporation	Owners have limited personal liability for business debts Fringe benefits can be deducted as business expense Owners can split corporate profit among owners and corporation, paying lower overall tax rate	More expensive to create than partnership or sole proprietorship Paperwork can seem burdensome to some owners Separate taxable entity

Ways to Organize Your Business (continued)		
Type of Entity	**Main Advantages**	**Main Drawbacks**
S Corporation	Owners have limited personal liability for business debts Owners report their share of corporate profit or loss on their personal tax returns Owners can use corporate loss to offset income from other sources	More paperwork than for a limited liability company, which offers similar advantages Income must be allocated to owners according to their ownership interests Fringe benefits limited for owners who own more than 2% of shares
Limited Liability Company	Owners have limited personal liability for business debts even if they participate in management Profit and loss can be allocated differently than ownership interests IRS rules allow LLCs to choose between being taxed as partnership or corporation	More expensive to create than partnership or sole proprietorship State laws for creating LLCs may not reflect latest federal tax changes

Deciding Who to Ask for Money

FORMS ON CD-ROM

Chapter 4 includes instructions for, and a sample of, the following form, which is in Appendix B and on the Loan Forms CD included at the back of this book:

- Best Bets List

I f your face were on the ten o'clock news, how many people would look up and say, "I know that person!"? The list is probably longer than you'd think—and includes more prospective lenders than you'd imagine. They need not be millionaires, and they need not be loyal relatives.

If you're like many small business owners, your first reaction to this book's topic may have been, "But I don't know enough people with money, much less people I'd feel comfortable asking for money." Don't let that initial reaction stop you. Asking people you know to pitch in on financing a new or growing business is anything but a radical idea. Before anyone had ever heard of banks, informal, person-to-person loans were the way many businesses got started—and the way many people made money.

> **TIP**
> **Be clear about how much money you need to borrow and when you can afford to pay it back (topics covered in Chapter 5).** This will help you best identify people who are good prospects.

Although modern banks have reduced the need for private financing, they haven't supplanted it. With approximately five out of every 100 adults in the United States having invested privately in someone else's business within the last three years, it's clear that private financing remains alive and well. It is, however, often hidden behind the doors of the family home. A whopping 42% of private investors are close family members, such as a spouse, sibling, child, parent, or grandparent. (*Source:* 2003 GEM study.) If you add in the 10% of investors who fall within the "other relative" category, that's more than half of all private investing coming from someone related to the entrepreneur.

Who Makes Private Investments	
Relationship of Investor to Entrepreneur	**Percentage of Private Investments**
Close family	42%
Other relative	10%
Work colleague	6%
Friend or neighbor	29%
Stranger	9%
Other	4%
Total	100%

But let's not overlook the fact that nearly half of private loans and investments come from people who are *not* related to the entrepreneur (29% friends and neighbors, and another 19% who are work colleagues, strangers, and others). Clearly, you should cast your mental net widely when thinking about your circle of contacts.

Chances are that you, like many entrepreneurs before you, will need to piece together business capital from several small loans and investments. Finding one person who can provide all the financing you need is unlikely and could be overly time consuming. To assemble your capital, you may need to both rekindle old relationships and start new ones. "Many of the most successful entrepreneurial ventures—those that create jobs, wealth, innovation, and economic growth—got off the ground because of the founder's ability to tap into his or her personal network for capital," says Carl J. Schramm, a leader in the field of entrepreneurship.

This chapter covers three main steps toward tapping into your network:

1. Brainstorming a list of the people you know.
2. Narrowing your list, based on trust, money, experience, and lack of emotional baggage.
3. Creating a summary "best bets" list.

Later chapters will show you how to make the most effective pitch and provide paperwork and information in an organized, business-like way, by setting up the loan and managing it with signed legal documents.

Brainstorming a List of Prospects

Your first step is simply to draw up a huge list of names, including your family, friends, colleagues, and beyond. You are in search of people with whom you already have, or can establish, a trusting relationship. You also want to identify people who are interested in seeing you succeed, either for personal or for business reasons.

TIP
Proper brainstorming involves not rejecting anyone who pops into your mind. Now is not the time to think about how remote your relationship to a particular person is, or how unlikely he or she is to loan you money—it's just time to make a list.

To make the process of thinking up names somewhat systematic, visualize the people you know as occupying three concentric circles. All three circles are in orbit around you, at the center of this mini-universe. (Just don't tell people that you think of them this way!) The innermost circle includes your nearest and dearest, the middle circle includes your other current relationships, and the outermost circle includes people with whom you aren't in direct, regular, or current contact.

It will be easiest to start your list with the people in your inner circle—those with whom you have the closest relationships. The obvious suspects include parents, grandparents, siblings, aunts, uncles, cousins, and in-laws, as well as close friends and neighbors—people you call or email regularly. Don't forget the relatives you rarely contact because you know you'll see them every year at Thanksgiving or at the beach.

The middle circle includes people with whom you are a bit more distant relationship-wise, but with whom you currently and regularly associate, particularly in the course of your professional life. These should be folks who think well of you because of what you do and how you do it. Think about business associates; fellow volunteers; members of your church, temple, or mosque; people with whom you've worked in current or past jobs; and supervisors or employers in those workplaces. If you're in business right now, consider which of your customers or suppliers really like what you do. Also think about any potential business mentors or entrepreneurs—people who may have good knowledge and information about the kind of business you're in, and whom you either know already or could get to know. Most of the contact information for people in this circle will likely be in your address book or computer.

Finally, the outermost circle reaches to folks with whom you've had contact in the past, friends or acquaintances you rarely see, and people you know only through someone else. These people should either know your name or recognize and think highly of a mutual acquaintance. Beyond your business experience, think back to teachers, college friends, mentors, professors, coaches, and others who might have an interest in seeing you succeed. If you happen to know any business angel investors—affluent individuals with experience and an interest in helping new businesses get started—add their names, too, if you haven't already. To come up with some names for this outermost circle, skim through your address book, email database, holiday greeting card list, old school yearbooks, alumni directories, employee rosters from old jobs, and even party invitation lists.

If your brainstormed list feels short, you might ask a trusted friend or colleague to help out. Your friend may either know of local people who have invested in other businesses or simply remember a mutual contact that you'd forgotten.

If you are an active user of a social networking website, such as Facebook or LinkedIn, it should not be too difficult to identify possible prospects from your contacts. You can also use these sites as a brainstorming tool to identify friends of friends and business associates who should be included on your prospect list.

Doctor, Lawyer ... Dentist Lenders?

Ahmet Ertegun grew up in a musical home and by the age of five had fallen in love with jazz. After graduate school, he and his friend Herb Aramson started a record label. When the first few albums didn't do well, they decided to sell the company and start over. They were unable to convince any of Ahmet's father's friends to invest, so they turned to Dr. Vahdi Sabit, the family dentist. Sabit put up $10,000 by mortgaging his house. Atlantic Records became one of the great soul labels in U.S. history and survives today as part of Time-Warner. (See www.history-of-rock.com/atlantic_records.htm and www.bsnpubs.com/atlantic/atlanticstory.html.)

Narrowing Your List

To turn your long list of contacts into a short list of prospects, evaluate each person in terms of the characteristics listed below. Circle the names of people who you feel can afford to lend you money and possess *at least two* of these characteristics:

- trust in you
- business experience, and
- lack of emotional baggage.

CAUTION

Don't choose a lender out of desperation. Although you need the money, don't go so far as to take it from people you don't trust or like. Aspiring café owner Andrea says, "I avoid people who only seem interested in the money part, and not in what it takes to grow the business; people who say they can't wait to tell 'their people' about the deal; or people who are pushy. It's a gut feeling ...."

Ability to Afford the Loan

The higher someone's net income is, the more likely this person is to agree to a loan. While it's great to have a long list of people who trust and adore you, the ones who can't spare the cash—or can't spare enough to make a difference—should simply be crossed off your list as prime prospects themselves. (They may end up having some useful contacts, so keep them on the list if that's the case.) If you're seeking to raise $75,000 and you know your fraternity brother can (at best) lend you $500, he should not be a prime prospect.

How do you figure out whether a person can afford to lend you money? You may know that the person has made a loan before, through gossip by family members or word-of-mouth among friends or colleagues. Observing the cars that people drive or the vacations they take can alert you to some who have money. (But watch out for the people who simply spend every dime of their income.) Other people are less showy in their behavior, and you may need to spend some time building the relationship to get a sense of their financial situation.

For each prospect on your list, ask yourself: "Can this person afford to lose the money?" It helps to secure the loan with your business or personal assets (as we explain in Chapter 9). But your lenders should still be able to say that losing the money wouldn't sink them financially. Andrea, who has been raising money from over 20 people to start her café, says that she has never and will never ask for money from someone she knows can't afford to lose it. It's simply one of the fundraising principles she's set for herself. If your older sister wants to help you start your home design business and is willing to dip into her kids' college fund, think twice if you don't think you can repay a $5,000 loan by the time your sister needs the money in four years.

Finally, finding people who can provide larger amounts means less work for you overall. Raising $50,000 in two $25,000 loans, for example, will require a lot less effort (both before and during the loan) than raising $50,000 through ten $5,000 loans.

CAUTION

Don't even think of borrowing from someone who relies on a limited, fixed income, such as Social Security. No matter how optimistic you feel about your business' chances for success, the risks aren't worth it—their income is too precious.

Trust in You

Identify those people who know your character or abilities and trust that your deeds will match your words. Family and friends with whom you have good relationships, and people with whom you've worked, especially your supervisors or employers, may fall into this category. Close friends and colleagues of your close contacts may also be good prospects.

People who are "control freaks" probably do not trust you, or their trust may come with a high price tag. (See "Avoiding the Control Freaks," below.) Of course, not every person who is willing to lend you money is a true control freak. (However, if you eventually attract equity investments from business angels, you should expect that they will exert a degree of financial control. It's part of being a shareholder in the business—they make the risky investment, so they deserve some insight and influence to help protect their investment.)

Avoiding the Control Freaks

Some lenders are the very opposite of self-sacrificing—their loans will come with strings attached. For example, they may want to have a say in running your business, or they may enjoy the power associated with having you become reliant on them. Even some parents and grandparents fall prey to this, perhaps as the natural result of paying for your diapers and food since day one. For other relatives, friends, and business associates, lending you money creates an opportunity to exert control over your life, your business, and your interactions with them.

A character on the classic TV show M*A*S*H—crusty, elitist Dr. Charles Winchester—comes to mind. In one episode, Dr. Winchester acts according to character when paychecks for his fellow doctors are delayed. He becomes a de facto loan shark, fronting his friends some cash, but expecting that each perform favors for him until he is repaid. If you know your prospects' personalities, you can probably predict which ones are the Dr. Winchesters and decide how to proceed accordingly. It's quite possible that you should not proceed with some of them at all.

Business Experience

People who are themselves entrepreneurs are the most likely to put money into other businesses. Perhaps the reason is that, as said in the GEM report: "They understand the entrepreneurial process; they are able to evaluate the prospects of another entrepreneur's venture; and they like to support other entrepreneurs with both money and advice."

Pundits say that the average successful entrepreneur has private investments in three other businesses, and the average successful senior-level corporate executive has investments in five other private ventures. So if you think that people who own their own business have their hands too full to lend to yours, think again. Your business may be just the extracurricular activity they're looking for.

Business experience is not a necessary characteristic for a lender. After all, the lender's level of involvement in your business is totally up to you. But knowledgeable supporters who can advise you based on their experience will prove invaluable.

Surveys Say That Your Best Bet Is ...

The most promising prospect for an informal investment is an older male relative, himself an entrepreneur, with high income and high net worth. Sounds stereotypical, and it may change in the future, but that's what the numbers currently show. Of course, your circle may not include anyone who fits this profile, and you may do just fine raising money from all types of people. But anyone in your circle who matches the description above should be at the top of your list.

No Emotional Baggage

Emotional baggage is the stuff that weighs people down. Review your list of business prospects to make sure there are no people with whom, in your gut, you feel nervous about entering a financial relationship. If you find any, cross them off the list.

Look for people who are comfortable mixing money and relationships and who aren't worried that loaning money for your business could damage your relationship or create problems with other relatives. We'll show you how to alleviate these concerns and avoid awkward interactions down the road with a carefully written promissory note laying out all the terms, including a realistic repayment plan covering missing and late payments.

Past conflict between you and the other person is the biggest red flag, especially if it remains unresolved. For example, if just last year you didn't speak to your brother for six months due to a misunderstood remark to his girlfriend, and your relationship is still a bit shaky, you should probably not consider him a prospect—not even if he has the money and related business experience to make him a good prospect. Similarly, you should not ask someone for money if you aren't on good terms with this person's spouse or partner. A loan can be a great source of friction within the home if the couple does not see eye to eye on it.

If asking one or both parents for money could cause tension in the family, avoid that as well. Many families do quite well at sharing their resources between generations (see "The Family Bank," below). But you know your family best. If you believe that the loan would only cause tension with your siblings and anxiety on the part of your parents, crossing them off your list at the beginning might be best.

Of course, very few relationships are perfect, and people can change. In some cases, a successful loan experience may represent a big step forward for a relationship.

> **EXAMPLE:** Cal was a recent college graduate with no savings or credit to speak of. His parents offered him the money he needed to launch his online business but he wanted to demonstrate his independence and refused to take the money as a gift. Instead, they agreed to formalize it as a loan, with a generous repayment structure. Cal borrowed $9,000, which for him was a lot of money. He made his payments on time even during the many months when he was cutting it close. For Cal, showing his parents he could be financially independent and responsible was just as important to him as getting the money he needed to launch his business.

Whatever you do, don't ignore relationship issues when considering whom to ask for money, particularly when it comes to family members. If the business fails, people will take sides, and things could get very uncomfortable. Be honest with yourself about whether the personal relationship can handle the financial risk of a an intrafamily loan.

Creating Your Best Bets List

Now let's take the remaining names on your list and create something more organized. Draw up a table that lists "Best Bets"—that is, people who can afford the money and have at least two of the characteristics described in the previous section. We include a sample below and a Best Bets List worksheet for this in Appendix B and on the Loan Forms CD at the back of this book. The list includes columns for the following information:

- each person's name
- a brief description of why the person appears to be a good prospect—altruism, self-interest, previous experience with private loans, or experience with small business start-ups (motivations discussed in Chapter 1's "What's in It for Your Family and Friend Lenders?")
- the best way to contact the prospect, and
- the target amount to request (how much you think you can ask for from a particular individual). You'll fill in this last column after you do the financial calculations discussed in Chapter 5.

Best Bets List

Prospect Name	Prospect Description	Contact Information	Amount to Request
Jane Smith	Mother, has money, trusts me, and we have a good, open relationship	Use home phone: 111-222-3333	
Joe Thompson	Uncle who started, managed, and sold his business; I think he might have invested in some other businesses of his golf buddies.	Use email or cell phone: joe@jt.com 111-333-4444	
Pete Williams	Friend from college; reconnected at reunion, turns out he's been very successful in the same industry that I'm trying to enter.	Dig up his business card from desk drawer: ____-____-____	

The Family Bank

If your parents or other elders are well off, you're probably not the only one in your generation hoping for a loan or other money transfer. Some families deal with the competing requests by adopting a "family bank" approach, in which the parents make loans available to all their children, on condition that the children agree to certain preset standards.

Family banks and similar concepts are not new ideas. They've been in use for many generations in some wealthy families. The family bank was particularly common before institutional lending and credit cards became prevalent. The point is to leverage the family's financial resources in a win-win transaction between family members—the children gain the use of the parents' money, and the interest payments stay within the family. The family bank can be a great source of help, but also a great source of friction if not properly managed.

To make family banks work for multiple loans within the same family, the lender should take the following steps:

- Treat each loan request with the same respect and analysis, by focusing on its financial merits.
- Keep everything in writing, as if the borrower and lender were strangers. Relying on people to remember the exact terms of their loan is a recipe for trouble.
- Establish some standards to which all loans must adhere, such as a minimum interest rate, a maximum loan amount, and required documentation.
- Keep each borrower's loan terms and status private. If the borrowers want to share information, that is their prerogative.
- Communicate to everyone involved the benefits that accrue to borrowers in good standing, such as lower interest rates and better repayment terms.
- Communicate to everyone the events that would trigger the "bank" to stop making loans in general, or to one person in particular.
- Consult with a family accountant or attorney on a regular basis to handle the tax implications of the family bank in general, and of each loan in particular.

TIP

Even after you've created your table of best prospects, don't discard any of your draft lists. Remember, this is just the first phase of a long process. You'll probably need to come back to your old drafts for more ideas later; see "Expanding Your Circle," below. Even the most distant contact that you wrote off during the first round could lead you to your next source of capital.

Expanding Your Circle

When I started raising money for CircleLending, I tapped out my list of best prospects pretty quickly. My business needed additional money to grow, and I had to both revisit my brainstorming list and come up with some new names. I asked people in my inner circle (both my investors and others I'd never even approached) whether they would each mind sharing the names of three contacts—relatives, friends, or business associates—whom they thought might be business angel investors.

A number of people agreed to think it over. By now, they'd heard me talking a lot about my new business and were happy to be asked for such an easy (and cheap!) way to participate. Nevertheless, getting back to me obviously wasn't the first thing on their minds, and I had to follow up in many cases. Within the next two years, my circle of new investor contacts grew considerably using this technique.

My former boss at a consulting company was just one of the people who helped in this effort. He had already made a small equity investment in my new business. Then, after I asked for his list of three, he introduced me to two of his associates, each of whom soon invested in the business as well. Later, as I built relationships with the two new investors and they grew to trust me and the business, each introduced me to new associates of theirs, prospects who amazingly led to even larger investments. All this from asking my former boss for a few names!

Preparing Your Business Plan and Your Fundraising Request

FORMS ON CD-ROM

    Chapter 5 includes instructions for, and samples of, the following forms, which are in Appendix B and on the Loan Forms CD included at the back of this book:

- Start-Up Costs Worksheet
- Recurring Costs Worksheet

The most effective way to ask for money for your business is to pitch—or sell—your idea, as you'll learn how to do in Chapter 8. But you can't sell someone on an idea that you haven't fully developed—and the established method for developing a business idea is to write a business plan, plotting out your business' immediate future in detail, and backing up your projections with researched facts and figures. Even the amount you ask people for will depend in part on the analysis within your plan.

If you were to apply for a bank loan, the loan officer would almost certainly ask to see your business plan. Even when it comes to private lenders (close friend or not), there's a very good chance that one of their first questions in response to your overtures will be, "Sounds interesting. Can I see a copy of your business plan?" Needless to say, having your plan ready and waiting is a sign that you literally mean business.

Don't make the mistake of thinking that a business plan is just a hoop through which you must jump to gain access to the business capital you need. It just so happens that a well-thought-out business plan is one of the best predictors of small business success—not because there's any magic in the paperwork itself, but because of the thinking and research that you will pour into it. Even a one-person business needs a business plan, modest as it may be.

The exercise of preparing a business plan, the focus of this chapter, will be an illuminating, and at times shocking, journey. It may help convince you that your idea is right on—or it may persuade you not to give up your day job. It will also help you figure out exactly how much money you need to raise and when you can realistically expect to pay it back. You'll then be in a strong position to start approaching your list of best bet prospects you developed in Chapter 4.

 TIP

Gift givers will also want to know you've thought out your business plan. Your parents and relatives will especially feel good that their gift money will be put to good use and that you have clear plans for your business.

The Perils of Jumping Without Looking

Faced with losing his job when his employer, the Common Ground Diner, announced its closing, Marty figured it was time to start his own business. Loyal customers were sad to see the diner go, and Marty felt that, as the diner's accountant and host for the past two years, he had the experience to make a new restaurant work. He and several other former employees found a property just a mile away and pooled their resources. One suggested they draw up a business plan, but Marty figured they would just pick up where the Common Ground Diner had left off. They were just $10,000 short of what they needed when Marty came up with the idea of asking some of the diner's most loyal customers to pitch in.

Marty remembered that a couple named Allen had been teary-eyed at their final meal at the Common Ground Diner. He invited the Allens for a coffee at the new property, energetically described his vision for a new place, and asked if they would be willing to help. The couple got back to Marty a week later. Their offer was by no means a sweet deal—$10,000 at 15% interest, to be repaid in 12 monthly payments. Marty balked at the size of the monthly payments. Realizing, however, that the cash would allow Marty's Place to open in time for tourist season, he accepted the deal and signed the promissory note.

Marty's Place opened as scheduled. But between rainy weekends and a road construction project around the corner, it just couldn't draw enough customers. The Allens began calling regularly, asking whether they were making any money yet. Marty made his first two payments but then was unable to keep up, which only increased the pace of the calls and began a series of tense and emotional drop-in visits.

As the weather turned colder, Marty's colleagues jumped ship. Marty, now unemployed, was left to liquidate the business's assets and pay off its debts as best he could. His father ended up bailing him out and paying off the loan to the Allens.

Without a business plan, Marty had gotten in over his head. Had he spent some time planning his business and working more in the restaurant industry, his venture might have had a different outcome. The Allens, too, were left with a bitter first experience with a private loan.

Recommended Business Planning Resources

There isn't space in this book to provide a complete discussion of how to write a business plan. For that, you should turn to the wealth of business plan preparation resources available to entrepreneurs, including:

- The U.S. Small Business Administration (SBA), at www.sba.gov, the federal agency charged with supporting small businesses (Chapter 2 describes SBA loan guarantee programs and business counseling services). Search the SBA website for "write a business plan" (or see www.sba.gov/smallbusinessplanner/plan/writeabusinessplan/index.html) and you'll find lots of free resources including an online workshop that takes you step-by-step through the process of preparing a business plan. Check out other resources on the SBA site, such as template forms for building financial statements (at www.sba.gov/tools/Forms/smallbusinessforms/fsforms/index.html).

- *Bplans*, created by Palo Alto Software Inc., at www.bplans.com. The website contains hundreds of sample business plans from dog kennels to wine stores and lots of advice on writing a business plan.

- *How to Write a Business Plan*, by Mike McKeever (Nolo), a comprehensive guide to writing a business plan—including how to evaluate the profitability of your business idea; estimate operating expenses; determine assets, liabilities, and net worth; and find potential sources of financing.

- SCORE, the nonprofit association with over 11,000 retired and working business executive volunteers who provide free business counseling and advice as a public service. The website (www.score.org) allows you to find a local SCORE counselor and access to a variety of financial spreadsheets and financial planning tools (see the "Business Tools" section at www.score.org/business_toolbox.html). SCORE's "Business Plan for a Startup Business" template (see www.score.org/pdf/Business_Plan_for_Startup_Business_08.pdf) provides a good starting point for writing a business plan.

Preparing Your Business Plan

There is no one way to write a business plan, nor any one format to put it in. Focus on putting together the most effective business plan for your needs in a way that is, paradoxically, both thorough and concise. Typical plans range from a few pages to over a hundred pages.

To get ideas, look at sample business plans for existing businesses in your industry (for example, on the www.bplans.com website). Draft your plan based on what you feel is effective—or flawed—in what you see. After creating a first draft, look to free small business counselors like the ones at your local SBA or SCORE office to review and provide comments on your plan, or check with an experienced business colleague.

 SKIP AHEAD

Already have a business plan you feel confident about? Skip ahead to "Calculating the Amount of Your Business Loan Request," below.

The main body of your business plan should include:
- a narrative (written) description of the business
- a financial description of the business, and
- supporting documents, such as your résumé or tax returns.

Once you've developed these sections, you'll also want to write an executive summary and a cover letter for your plan. Although these are the last things you'll prepare, they are the first and most important sections any prospect will look at.

Drafting the Narrative Description

The narrative section of your business plan is the place where you communicate the opportunity you see and the business you plan to build in response, as well as describe the product or service you will offer, the market, the competition, and the people who will make it all happen. Try to be as compelling as possible, backed up with real numbers.

Business opportunity. Try beginning with a problem statement and then presenting your business as a solution. For example, you might explain that a local airport lacks shuttle service and how you will fill this gap. If you have already started your business, cite any of its accomplishments to date, such as the number of customers served, products sold, or contracts received. These show that you have gained some traction or momentum in solving the problem. Lenders will be particularly interested in knowing that you have real, live customers; how many you have; how much they pay you; and how you'll get more.

Operating plan. Provide a simple overview of how your business operates. If you will make a product, describe the process through which you will acquire your materials and create the product. If you will sell a service, describe your activities behind the scenes and in dealing with customers. For example, if you plan to analyze data freely available from the U.S. government and then sell your analysis, describe how you will get the raw data, what the analysis will include, what you will produce, and how you will package and deliver it (perhaps as a printed report, CD-ROM, or downloadable file) to your customers.

Pay attention to the implication of your operating plan on your cash flow. Make sure that you've thought through the timing of when you will receive payments (cash inflow) and when you will need to pay for things (cash outflow). Making sure you have enough cash on hand when the bills come due is one of the biggest challenges many entrepreneurs face.

Market analysis. Do your best to quantify the opportunity you have identified. Estimate the size of your market in numbers and dollar figures. Show who the customers are by giving some demographic information (see "Compiling Demographic Information on Your Customers and Clients," below), and describing how you plan to reach them, including online. Also explain why you think these customers will buy from you or use your service.

Compiling Demographic Information on Your Customers and Clients

Knowing who your customers are and what motivates them to pick your product or service over a competitor's is an important part of your business plan. Do your best to describe the people most likely to patronize your business. Do they fall into a certain age group, geographic pattern, gender, interest group, or ethnic group? For example, if you believe that your new magazine will appeal most to older, female churchgoers in your region, then you can tailor your marketing strategy accordingly. (You will probably need to find methods of communication that reach that group, such as particular newsletters, radio shows, or events you can sponsor.)

Test your demographic theories by talking to owners of similar businesses in similar geographic areas (you may be able to get some good leads from trade associations and media reports). If you've already floated a start-up or test version of your business, talk to or survey your existing customers. Then, collect information on how many people fit your target audience, with help from your local reference librarian and the U.S. Census Bureau (www.census.gov). The "Business" section of the Bureau's website includes economic statistics on a variety of topics, including the income levels of the people in your area and the number of businesses in your sector and industry.

Competition. Don't kid yourself; someone else out there is probably already doing what you want to do. Identify who they are, then figure out why your product or service is better. Companies compete primarily on two fronts: cost (who charges the least) and quality (whose product or service is the best). Depending upon the service or the product, location and convenience can also be important factors. Be honest about whom you are up against, and state clearly why you will be the one to win the customers. And don't forget to include the costs of winning those customers. (*Marketing Without Advertising*, by Michael Phillips & Salli Raspberry (Nolo) provides lots of ideas for high-impact, lost-cost marketing.)

Personnel. Provide brief biographies of yourself and any key employees. Include your education and work experience. Highlight any training and professional experience specific to your industry or to starting and running a business.

Preparing the Financial Description

Like it or not, you will need to understand and present your business in financial terms to be successful. This section provides only a summary of the financial terms and statements that are critical for entrepreneurs to understand and use. If these are not yet familiar to you, consult additional resources and get advice from a business counselor or adviser. While you can hire a good accountant to help you get started, that doesn't let you off the hook completely. You personally will need to be able to tell the story of your business idea with numbers—and to make sure that the numbers tell as compelling a story as your narrative does.

The following section explains how to do this by preparing a Sources and Use of Funds table. If you're already earning some money by selling your product or service, prepare the following materials (with the help of your accountant as necessary):

- three standard financial statements, including a cash flow statement, and
- spreadsheets, including a break-even analysis, that show how your business will grow.

These tables and spreadsheets deal in projected, not actual, figures but are a critical piece of the planning puzzle for anyone considering lending you money.

 SEE AN EXPERT

Look for a good, local accountant to help you set up effective financial and management systems and get you going on the right software package for your business. Being able to generate accurate and timely records will be crucial to your ability to understand your business, make mid-course corrections, and generate the reports and records lenders might require. At this early stage, you don't need an expensive accounting firm; you need someone who is affordable and who has experience helping businesses like yours get off the ground.

Putting Your Request Into Numbers With a Sources and Uses of Funds Table

At the beginning of your business plan's financial description, you should include what's known as a Sources and Uses of Funds table. The purpose of this table is to let your prospect know exactly how much you are raising overall, whom you are raising it from, and what the money will be spent on. See the sample below, for a fictional company called "ABC Business."

The "Uses of Funds" portion of the table will show how much business capital you are attempting to raise, by detailing what you need it for and how much each item costs. The Sources of Funds portion of the table shows where you plan to raise the capital from and how much will come from each source. Make sure the total Uses of Funds figure matches the total Sources of Funds figure.

Sources and Uses of Funds Table: ABC Business

Sources of Funds:

Personal savings	$ 5,000
Personal line of credit	12,000
To be raised from private loans	10,000
Total	$ 27,000

Uses of Funds:

Two trucks @ $12,000	$ 24,000
Recurring costs for six months @ $500/month	3,000
Total	$ 27,000

Portraying Existing Business Activities Numerically on Financial Statements

As a business owner, you must become familiar with the three standard financial statements that show what's going on with your business: the balance sheet, income statement, and cash flow statement. All existing businesses generate these three financial statements on a quarterly basis and at the end of each fiscal year (annually). Some also do it monthly. You can find templates—spreadsheets you can fill out with your own figures—on the SBA and SCORE websites (see "Recommended Business Planning Resources," above).

Balance sheet. This financial statement shows a summary of your business' assets (what you own) and liabilities (what you owe). It's a snapshot in time. In other words, the statement is used to communicate the financial condition of a business at any one point—for example, at the end of a quarter or the end of a fiscal year.

Income statement. This monthly or quarterly statement shows how much your business actually earned after your expenses were all paid out that period.

Cash flow statement. This monthly or quarterly statement shows where your business' cash came from and where it went during the period.

Projecting Future Business Plans Numerically

Even existing businesses include projections in their business plans. People who lend or give you money are even more interested in the future of the business than they are in its past and want to see what story the numbers tell about the future growth you have in mind. The bulk of the financial description of your business plan will be financial projections.

Financial projections are spreadsheets that show projections—in other words, your best guesstimates—of the finances of your business anywhere from a few months to several years into the future. The two most common types of projections to include in your business plan are a break-even analysis and pro forma financials.

Break-even analysis. This analysis shows how much income you'll need to earn to cover your expenses. After that point, your income will presumably increase faster than your expenses, and your business will begin turning a profit. If you don't have a break-even analysis already, you can create one for your business online, at the SCORE website. (From the Business Toolbox, go to the Template Gallery, where you will find over a dozen forms including a break-even analysis form that you can fill in and adjust to match your own business situation.)

Pro forma financials. These are simply any of the three standard financial statements, projected into the future. The figures that appear in pro formas are projections of how the business *thinks* it will perform on each item. These projections usually extend out for three years. They force you to detail the economics of your business and how an event, such as an increase in the cost of a raw material or a lowering of tax rates, will affect your bottom line. Experienced lenders may review your pro formas to see whether you understand the economics of your own business and whether you've been realistic in projecting its future. Several templates are available at the SCORE website mentioned above. The "Profit and Loss Projection (12 Months)" is a particularly common one to include in a start-up business plan.

Supplying Supporting Documents

Because most of the material presented in your plan reflects your subjective opinion of your business, it's important to provide some objective backup to your other reports. Helpful supporting documents usually include, but are not limited to:

- tax returns
- copies of any contracts, leases, licenses, or letters of intent, and
- your résumé and the résumés of your key employees.

If you're just getting started, you obviously won't have tax returns. And if you're starting on a small scale, you may not have signed any contracts or leases. Do your best to think of equivalent items that will show that you're serious about starting this business, or that others have expressed an interest in participating or buying from you. For example, if you have a prospective customer who could be a significant buyer, such as another business, you could try to get the customer to put into writing his or her interest in buying a certain amount of your product at a certain price. This isn't a legal agreement, simply a letter of interest you can show to potential lenders (and equity investors, later, should you come to that point).

Drafting an Executive Summary

A good plan includes an executive summary, usually no longer than one page, capturing the highlights of the plan. While it's easiest to wait until *after* you've drafted your business plan to create your executive summary, it should be positioned *before* the plan when you package it up for others to see. In some circumstances, the executive summary can serve as a standalone document, such as when you need something short and sweet to share with a prospect.

To draft the executive summary, refer back to the narrative description of your business, and pull the strongest points from each section. Use the same headings, but use just the few sentences or one paragraph that conveys the most important (and persuasive) information from that section. Extract financial highlights that best illustrate the opportunity, such as a projected profit margin or a pending contract. If you have a particularly powerful table, logo, or graphic, use it. The bplans.com website has executive summaries you can review to get a sense of how to write your own.

TIP

Make your executive summary an attention grabber. Lenders will always read the summary first, because it's the shortest description of the business. They will continue to the details only if they find the summary compelling.

Adding a Cover Letter

When you ultimately share your plan with others, always include a cover letter prepared for each person and occasion. Include your contact information on the letter and an encouragement that readers contact you with any questions.

Calculating the Amount of Your Business Loan Request

Don't make the mistake that many entrepreneurs do, and simply raise as much—or as little—as you think your lenders can part with. Another common mistake is to think that if you can just raise enough for that one piece of equipment and your first month of lease payments, that the rest will take care of itself. Instead, you'll need to figure out exactly how much money you'll need to start or expand your business and to keep it running for as many months as it takes until you find customers and get established. You can calculate this amount in three easy steps:

Step 1: Identify and total your predicted start-up (or expansion) costs.

Step 2: Identify and total your predicted recurring costs.

Step 3: Total the two figures from Steps 1 and 2.

The three sections below will guide you through these steps. You'll also find copies of the relevant worksheets in Appendix B and on the Loan Forms CD that you can edit for your own business needs. Most entrepreneurs will be able to estimate their start-up costs on their own, using one of these tools. However, if you are already in business, or you have a complex array of income and expenses to estimate, you may need some help from a small business adviser or accountant.

TIP
You'll probably need more money than you think. Many entrepreneurs underestimate how much money they'll need to get their new business off the ground. Take the time to understand how your business will

both earn and use cash. When you make projections (in your business plan and in the Start-Up Costs Worksheet described below), be conservative. Pay particular attention to the ability of your business to make a profit; that's where most entrepreneurs go wrong—by being overly optimistic. Consider creating three sets of projections: "best case," for how you hope things will work out; "base case," for how you can confidently predict things will progress based on current information; and "worst case," assuming 50% or less of your base case scenario.

Step 1: Estimating Your Start-Up Costs

Estimate the start-up costs you will incur prior to your first day of business. These include one-time expenses you will have to pay before you can open your doors. The list in the table below will give you an idea of what to include. Use the "Other" line for items unique to your situation. Calculate a total at the bottom.

Start-Up Costs Worksheet

Description	Estimated cost
Legal fees	$
Rent (include deposit and first month)	$
Office equipment	$
Insurance (initial premium)	$
Business license	$
Stationery, logos, letterhead	$
Initial advertising	$
Other	$
Total start-up costs	$

Step 2: Estimating Your Recurring Costs

Estimate the costs you will incur on a regular (usually monthly) basis regardless of what happens with your business. For example, you'll have to pay your monthly rent no matter how many widgets you create to fill your orders, or how much income your business generates.

Describe the basis for the cost in the description column. For monthly costs, record the dollar amount in the second column. For costs that occur less regularly—for example, quarterly insurance payments or annual trade association dues—divide the cost up into a monthly amount, and include that as well. Total all the rows in the second column to find out your total recurring monthly costs.

Recurring Costs Worksheet

Description	Estimated monthly cost
Monthly rent	$
Payroll	$
Utilities	$
Insurance	$
Ongoing advertising	$
Association and other memberships	$
Other	$
Total monthly recurring costs	$

Step 3: Calculating Total Funds Needed

The last step is to combine the start-up costs (Step 1) and the recurring costs (Step 2) to get the total amount you'll need to raise for your business. But before you can do this, you need to determine how many months of recurring costs to add.

Figure out how many months it will take you to find customers and get established. Some entrepreneurs will want to plan their finances all the way to the month when they expect to break even (where income meets expenses). If you created a break-even analysis as part of your business plan, refer back to it for this figure. Some entrepreneurs pick an arbitrary number like three, six, or 12 months, knowing they may need to raise additional capital down the road. Think carefully about how many months of costs you will incur before you can earn enough revenue that you don't need outside money to make ends meet.

Total Funds Worksheet

Total of your start-up costs (from Step 1)		$ _____
Recurring costs (from Step 2)	$ _____	
Number of months	x _____	
Total recurring costs	=	$ _____
Total funds needed		$ _____

Once you have calculated the total amount needed to launch your business, subtract from it any funds you have already raised. For example, if you plan to use a line of credit you have with a bank, decide how much you can use from that source. If you're planning on using money from your personal savings, subtract that amount as well. The amount you're left with is the amount you'll need to raise from your prospects.

Dividing Up Your Request Among Prospects

Now you know how much money you want to raise in total. The next step is to divide up that amount into smaller parts and write down a likely dollar figure, or a range, next to each name on your prospects list. Don't worry about being too exact—these numbers will probably change as you discuss the request with each prospect. The point here is to get to an amount that you can use when you first approach a prospect—an amount you've picked for good reason, not pulled from thin air. Pick one of the following three ways to divide up the total:

- Ask for all the money from one person.
- Ask for the same amount from several people.
- Ask for different amounts from different people.

If, no matter which way you slice it, the total amount you think you can request from your prospects falls short of what you'll need for your business, go back and reconsider the people you crossed off your brainstorming list in Chapter 4. Also, go back to your business plan to see if there are any areas where you can cut expenses or increase income, in order to lower the total cost you need to borrow.

Asking for All the Money From One Person

The first possibility, asking for all the money from one person, has both pros and cons. The pro is that it makes your life a lot easier if you have to manage a financial relationship with only one person. The con is that, from the lender's perspective, it might feel risky to be the sole person providing cash for your venture (assuming one person is in a position to lend you as much money as you need—or for as long a term as you need it). Spreading the request out among several people reduces the burden on each one. In the early stage, it also gives you alternatives in case you get turned down.

Asking for the Same Amount From Each Person

You might ask for the same amount from each prospect if you really don't know much about individual financial situations. Rather than spending time trying to guess or asking around about your prospects, it might be simpler and easier to ask for the same amount from each, especially if it's just a few thousand dollars.

An advantage of this option is that it can make your life easy. For example, if you need to borrow only $6,000 and you have three well-off prospects, asking for $2,000 from each allows you to use the same loan request letter, and possibly even the same loan terms. For those who say yes, promissory notes will be easy to prepare, because they'll be virtually the same.

> **TIP**
>
> **If you're raising money from several people, don't promise to pay them all on the same day each month.** It's smarter to space out the payments to come due at different times of the month, so you don't set yourself up to have everything due at once. The exception would be if you're confident that the payments are small enough that dealing with them simultaneously won't be a problem.

Asking for Different Amounts From Different People

The obvious disadvantage to the second option is that it doesn't take into account what you know about your prospects' individual financial situations. If your uncle could spare $5,000 and your book club pal would be more comfortable with $1,000, why ask both for $3,000? It doesn't take a lot of work to divide your total into differing amounts based on what you know about each individual prospect.

Selecting a range of possible loan amounts (for example, between $1,000 and $4,000) is fine as well. When the time comes to make the request, such an approach allows you to suggest the range and let the prospect pick the actual amount.

> **TIP**
>
> **It's often best to let the prospect pick the final amount.** Instead of guessing that your grandmother could lend you $8,000, put her on your list for $5,000 to $10,000. Then let her nail down the exact dollar figure. To some prospects it just plain feels better to suggest the amount of the investment, instead of merely agreeing to an amount that has been decided for them in advance.

Putting It All Together

Now fill in the fourth column (Amount to Request) of the Best Bets List you created in Chapter 4. Using the strategies described above, enter the amount of money you believe you can realistically ask of each person, either as a gift or a loan.

Best Bets List

Prospect Name	Prospect Description	Contact Information	Amount to Request
Jane Smith	Mother, has money, trusts me, and we have a good, open relationship	Use home phone: 111-222-3333	$20,000
Joe Thompson	Uncle who started, managed, and sold his business; I think he might have invested in some other businesses of his golf buddies.	Use email or cell phone: joe@jt.com 111-333-4444	$50,000
Pete Williams	Friend from college; reconnected at reunion, turns out he's been very successful in the same industry that I'm trying to enter.	Dig up his business card from desk drawer: ____-____-____	$5,000

Deciding Interest Rate, Repayment Schedule, and Other Loan Terms

FORMS ON CD-ROM

    Chapter 6 includes instructions for, and a sample of, the following form, which is in Appendix B and on the Loan Forms CD included at the back of this book:

- Collateral List

Reprinted with permission of Dave Swann and the Honolulu Star-Bulletin.

I f you're a "let's get this over with" type, you might—now that you've
got your business plan and know the amount you need to raise and
whom you're most likely to raise it from—be tempted to just pick
up the phone. Don't. You risk sounding only slightly more professional
than the fellow in the cartoon above if you approach your prospect
before you've thought through key elements of your loan request and are
ready to both answer questions and offer written materials spelling out
the details.

SKIP AHEAD

**This chapter is focused on requesting financing in the form of
a loan.** If you're planning to raise all or some money in the form of a gift, see
Chapter 11 which covers gifts.

In the world of banks and other institutional lenders, your loan
options would mostly be limited to particular interest rates, repayment

plans, and the like—take 'em or leave 'em. With a private loan, however, you have the opportunity to custom design a loan that works for you. But you must also take into account what your lender may want from the deal, particularly if your lender isn't entirely comfortable making the loan. For example, your nearest and dearest may be eager to loan you money for no collateral and at zero interest. More distant lenders, however, may not agree to a loan until you offer better-than-market-rate interest and a piece of business equipment as collateral.

By the way, I'm not yet talking about creating any written materials to show a prospective lender (that will come in Chapter 7 when you draft a loan request letter), although you should keep some fairly detailed notes for later use. The idea now is that either when you first approach a prospective lender, or during the discussions that follow soon thereafter, you'll be ready to tell the person:

- whether or not the loan will be secured with collateral
- what interest rate or range of rates you can offer, and
- how you will repay the loan and payment logistics.

Doing your homework now is crucial to making a pitch for a business loan (the topic of Chapter 8). We'll get to that soon. It's not that calling your prospects is taboo. In fact, after you've done the homework described in this chapter, a simple phone call, email, or other quick contact, may be just the ticket to opening communication channels between you and your prospective lender. However, flat out asking for the money now—without having done some important background work—practically guarantees that you will be turned down.

> **TIP**
>
> **Start by envisioning your ideal or typical loan; you can customize it to individual lenders later.** You might even use this chapter to draft alternate sets of loan terms, which you'll ultimately choose between or offer as options to lenders. The important thing is that you run the numbers and figure out your own needs and limits now—how much you can afford to pay over what time period—before a lender asks you any probing questions.

Different Terms for Different Lenders

When Soo-Kiat needed $10,000 to start a technology business in his university's business incubator, he first turned to his uncle. His uncle generously proposed a $5,000 interest-free loan, to be paid back over the course of three years. Soo-Kiat accepted. However, he still needed another $5,000.

Soo-Kiat's list of best prospects included several business school professors and a former employer. To make his loan request tempting to these savvy and analytical investors, Soo-Kiat put together a package with three loan options:

- a 10% interest rate on a 12-month loan of $2,500
- a 12% interest rate on an 18-month loan of $2,500
- a 15% interest rate on a 12-month loan of $5,000.

Notice that all three options had short repayment periods and high interest rates. This was intended as compensation for the fact that Soo-Kiat had no assets with which to secure the loan. He knew the prospects wouldn't operate based on the same altruistic motives as his uncle.

Soo-Kiat's strategy worked. Two prospects from his list agreed; one chose the first option, the other chose the second. Over the next three years, his business earned enough to keep up with each of his three repayment plans (from his uncle and the two other lenders) and to pay himself a respectable salary.

Will You Offer Collateral?

Here's another reason not to mourn if a bank or other traditional lender turns down your application for a loan. You can practically count on banks requiring you to secure their interests by providing collateral or security (property, such as your house or business assets, which the bank could sell if you failed to make your payments). The only form in which such traditional lenders might make an unsecured loan to a new business is by offering you a high-interest credit card. By contrast, as you'll see below, the majority of interpersonal loans are unsecured.

Even Family Might Require Collateral

After being turned away by several banks, Bill asked his father to lend him money to launch Neighborhood Transmission Services, a Los Angeles-based AAMCO franchise that provides automotive parts, transmission services, and general repairs. "The banks were reluctant to even consider my proposal," said Bill, and "the third-party financing I did manage to find carried exorbitant rates."

Bill's father agreed to a $20,000 loan with a two-year term, but on the condition that it be secured by the new company's assets. "I love Bill, but this is a business deal," said his father. He took a security interest in most of the shop equipment, including the most valuable part, the shop's new hydraulic lift.

"Private lending was a unique fit for what we needed," added Bill. "We were able to set up a quarterly payment structure, with an interest rate that was workable both for my father and my company." The loan is still in active repayment and the security provision has not needed to be exercised. Both parties hope it never needs to be.

Why Most Private Loans Are Unsecured

Friends and relatives tend to accept unsecured loans because they know your character and trust you to follow through on your promises. In fact, some private lenders would actually prefer that you not provide any collateral. They reason that your relationship will suffer if, for example, you offer up your home as collateral and then default on your loan. That would put your lender in the awful position of deciding whether to sell your home out from under you in order to collect.

TIP

Not sure whether collateral will reassure or alarm your family member? When planning to request a loan from a family member, start by assuming that an unsecured loan will satisfy his or her needs. The trust level between you and your relative is likely high enough that you won't need to put your personal or business assets at risk. You can always mention the possibility of attaching security to the loan later, if it seems appropriate after the two of you talk things over.

Of course, I've recommended that you cast your net widely when looking for potential lenders, and some of your prospects may be less interested in preserving your relationship than in protecting their money with a security interest. If that's at all foreseeable, your next task is to decide what you will offer as collateral. ·

What to Offer as Collateral

If you plan to offer a secured loan to your prospective lenders, you'll need to come up with a list of the property you are willing to give up if you can't repay (this will be part of the promissory note and security agreement we discuss in Chapter 9). I've known entrepreneurs to offer up everything from manufacturing equipment to their inventory of variety store goods. If you plan to get multiple loans, be sure to avoid pledging the same collateral on more than one loan. This could land you into trouble if the loans default and could prevent you from seeking institutional loans in the future.

Creating this collateral list isn't exactly fun: It means considering the failure of your business and your default on the private loan. However, as an entrepreneur, you've hopefully either learned to live with risk, or you feel certain that you'll find a way to repay the loan whether or not your business is a roaring success.

And you can take some comfort from the fact that, even if you do agree to a secured loan and you ultimately can't pay it, your friends and family probably won't resort to selling off your collateral. Although I've seen many cases of secured loans made between family members, including a fair number in which the borrower later had trouble repaying, I can think of only a handful in which the family members went so far as to exercise their security interest and liquidate the borrower's assets. More typically, if the borrower is teetering towards default, the family member will agree to restructure the payment schedule or accept deferred payments, topics discussed in Chapter 10.

Business Assets as Collateral

Nevertheless, you'll want to choose your collateral carefully, just in case a distant friend or a Scrooge-like family member exercises the option to foreclose. The following types of business assets are commonly used as collateral to secure a business loan:

- office equipment, such as computers, printers, copiers, phones, faxes, and furniture
- business equipment, such as manufacturing equipment, machinery, and tools
- vehicles, such as trucks, bulldozers, and forklifts
- real estate
- contracts, such as government orders for goods or services
- inventory, such as raw materials or in-process or finished goods
- accounts receivable, that is, records of people who owe money to your business
- investments owned by your business, such as marketable securities, CDs, bonds, and T-bills, and
- purchase orders.

If you don't have any—or enough—of these assets available to you, you may still find creative ways to use other, less-tangible types of business assets as collateral. For example, you could offer to assign the remainder of your prepaid lease to your lender. Similarly, you could assign a line of credit, patents, or name recognition and brand loyalty to your lender. Although these are hard to value, they do represent a source of economic value to your business.

CAUTION

Will you be offering any items of collateral that will depreciate in value as they age? If so, your lender may want you to factor this into your agreement. Most computers, for example, are now considered old after 18 to 24 months, so they should be used only for loans of a shorter length. If your lender chooses, you may need to develop a schedule documenting how much the computer will be worth for each year that it is being used to secure the loan. In addition, some lenders will want a provision put into the agreement allowing them to ask that new collateral be put up partway through the life of the loan if the original asset becomes worth less than the remainder of the loan.

Personal Assets as Collateral

If your business assets are insufficient to provide adequate collateral, you can also turn to your personal assets, such as:

- your house, land, or other real estate
- bank accounts
- investments, such as marketable securities, CDs, bonds, and T-bills, and
- vehicles.

Other personal assets you might put to work as collateral include your share of a family-owned piece of property. Or you might assign your rental deposit (held by your landlord) or some other type of deposit held by an unrelated third party. I probably don't have to remind you of the risks of putting your personal assets on the line—on the other hand, enduring some personal risk is often a necessary part of the entrepreneurial life.

How to Prepare Your Collateral List

Once you have a good idea of the business or personal items that might work as collateral, draw up a list containing a description and the approximate value of each, like the sample below (also available as a blank template in Appendix B and on the Loan Forms CD at the back of this book). Make your best guess at the value of your assets; you shouldn't need to actually have them appraised unless your lender asks you to.

Sample Collateral List

Item Description	Approximate Value
Business Assets	
Machinery	$12,000
Van	10,000
Accounts receivable	1,200
Personal Assets	
Home equity	$45,000
Car	15,000

Next, identify which of these assets you are willing to offer as collateral for a secured loan. Traditionally, the borrower offers a menu of assets for collateral, and the lender gets to decide which ones are sufficient to secure the loan. Your lender may pick just one asset, as token collateral to keep you on your toes, or may "over collateralize" the loan, asking for a security interest in assets whose values add up to more than the loan itself. While this may not seem fair, it's up to your lender to decide how much collateral he or she needs in order to feel that the loan is secure or safe. Then, it's up to you to decide how much you need the person's money, given the strings the lender has attached.

Paperwork Involved With Collateral

Using collateral will require extra paperwork. Much later, after you've agreed to a loan and are drawing up the documents for it, your promissory note will need to discuss and describe any collateral you've promised, in what's called a "security" or "secured interest provision." You'll also need to prepare and sign a document called a "security agreement." Finally, you'll need to file documents (called a UCC Financing Statement) to publicly record the security interest, with a state or county office. Chapter 9 provides more information on all these steps and the necessary forms.

> **TIP**
> **Collateral is not the lender's only backup if you borrow money and do not repay it.** The lender still has the option to sue you, get a court judgment, and then take money or property that can legally be seized to satisfy a debt.

How Much Interest Are You Willing to Pay?

To the inexperienced borrower, arriving at an interest rate may feel like pulling a number out of a hat. However, the process can be approached more scientifically.

Start with the Applicable Federal Rate (AFR) as your base. This is the rate set by the IRS as a minimum for private loans—use anything less and the IRS will consider the difference between your rate and the AFR to be a gift and will impute interest on it, putting your lender at risk of gift tax liability. (Refer back to Chapter 3, "Tax Liability If You Pay Too Little Interest," for this discussion.)

The AFR changes monthly, but not drastically. To give you an idea, between mid-2008 and mid-2009, the short-term (less-than-three-year loan term) AFR ranged between approximately 1% and 3%. To see the latest rate, visit the IRS website at www.irs.gov and search for "AFR." Then, using the drop-down index, select the current month and year.

Offering to pay the relatively low AFR probably isn't going to make the person jump with joy. To figure out how high above the AFR you should go, consider the alternatives available to both you and your lender. What interest rate would you have to pay to get money from another source? On the other side of the negotiating table, what return could your lender be earning elsewhere? You want to arrive at a number that lets both you and your lender feel like you're getting a good deal.

Most of the business borrowers I've worked with lately end up paying around 7%, although some have gone as low as the AFR and others as high as 15%. But before you choose, let's look at both your and your lender's competing alternatives in more detail.

TIP

If you will be paying interest, use simple (not compounded) interest to determine the amount of annual interest that you will owe on the loan. To figure out how much this will be, multiply the amount of the loan by the annual interest. For example, if you are borrowing $5,000 at 8% interest, the annual interest rate on the loan is $400. For a five-year loan, the total interest due would be $2,000. (This information will be detailed in your repayment schedule, not spelled out in the promissory note.)

Researching the Interest Rate You'd Pay Elsewhere

On the open market you're likely to pay interest at the same rate as credit cards or loans from banks, credit unions, or other financial institutions.

Your credit card rate. Over two-thirds of U.S. small businesses use a credit card for business purchases. The interest rate you'd pay to do this depends entirely on your personal and business credit. Look for the annual percentage rate (APR) noted on your personal or business card monthly statement to find out how much you'd pay if you used that card for your business' start-up expenses. Introductory rates can be 0% or very low, but watch out; those are usually just bait to reel you in. After the first six months, credit card rates often skyrocket to 20% or more (and higher if you include fees). (However, if you can pay off the debt within the six-month period, you've beaten the credit card company at its own game.)

Your local bank rates. Over half of all U.S. small businesses use commercial loans, lines of credit, or other financial services from banks. Small, creditworthy businesses that borrow from banks currently pay, on average, about an 8% interest rate. But remember, banks rely heavily on your personal and business credit rating, as well as the financial performance of your business, to determine the interest rate they'll offer you. The weaker your credit or business performance, the higher your interest rate.

If you want to know exactly how much a bank loan will cost you, submit an application. You can do so either online to a large lender to small businesses, like Bank of America, or in person, at your local bank. Many lenders will probably start discussing one of the SBA loan programs. For example, under the SBA 7(a) program, bank lenders pick the rate to offer borrowers, but it cannot exceed the prime rate plus 4.75% (equaling 8% as of July 2009; see the "Interest Rates Under the SBA 7(a) Loan Program" table in Chapter 2) for a loan of less than $25,000 with a loan term greater than seven years.

An alternative financial intermediary, such as a nonprofit lender or credit union. These sources of capital are willing to take on more risk—for example, by lending to borrowers who've been turned down by traditional banks due to a spotty credit history. These sources are also willing to lend smaller amounts than banks. However, nonprofit lenders and credit unions often charge commensurately higher interest rates, to compensate for this added risk and flexibility. One nonprofit I know of charged interest rates between 10% and 15%. Although this might sound exorbitant, the group was quite successful in helping many small businesses get off the ground—businesses that might otherwise not have started or grown, because others weren't willing to take a chance lending to them.

Researching the Interest Rate Your Prospects Could Get Elsewhere

If you're going to wow your prospective lenders with your professionalism, you'll need to show them that you're aware of the competition for their money and can preferably meet or exceed the going rates. These rates all change daily. The best way to find them easily and for free is at www.bankrate.com. However, I've included the rates from around the time this book was written (summer 2009), below. Use these as ballpark figures and to get an idea of the categories that you'll eventually need to look up.

Your various sources of competition for your prospect's money include:

- **Money market accounts.** These earned about 1.3% in the summer of 2009.

- **CDs (certificates of deposit).** Look for the CD with the term (length) that matches the term you plan to offer in your loan request. A one-year CD was earning 2.3%, and a five-year CD was earning 3% in the summer of 2009.
- **An account at ING.** This Web-based firm offers some of the most competitive rates available—1.5% in the summer of 2009 (www. ingdirect.com).

It's not too hard to offer better-than-market rates if your loan is short term (less than three years). For example, the above short-term investment options currently are paying at or below the AFR, so by simply meeting the present IRS minimum you would beat them. But for prospects to be attracted to a risky proposition, particularly without taking a security interest in your assets, you may need to offer lenders a significantly higher return on their money, something more in the 5% to 12% range.

Researching Your State's Limits (Usury Laws) on Interest Rates

Even if you're feeling wildly generous and want to pay your lenders interest rates in the 20%-and-up range, your state's usury laws may forbid it. Most states exclude loans for business purposes from the reach of these laws, but some don't. Usury laws were enacted to protect borrowers from exorbitantly high interest rates, on the assumption that the lenders hold all the cards. If a situation arises where your lender is found to be charging you a usurious rate (even if you suggested it), your lender could be forced to repay any excess monies they received, lower the interest rate to the highest rate allowed by state law for any future payments, and pay additional civil penalties for violating your state's usury laws.

If your lender is someone you know, he or she probably won't try to charge you an absurdly high interest rate, and I doubt you'll suggest it yourself. In any case, as a general rule of thumb, most states allow lenders to charge you up to 15% interest per year without running afoul of the usury law. Still, the usury limit varies widely from state to state, and different rules usually apply to commercial lenders and private lenders. Check your state's laws to be sure; look under "interest" or "usury" in your state's statutes, which are accessible through the Nolo website at www.nolo.com/legal-research.

Arriving at an Interest Rate That Satisfies Both Borrower and Lender

Once you've done your research, it shouldn't be hard to settle on a range of interest rates that will satisfy both you and your lender—for example, between 3% and 8%. Rates in this range could realistically be lower than you'd be able to get for a small business loan from traditional sources, yet higher than your lender would be able to earn for a short-term cash investment with a commercial entity like a bank. Settling on a range like this is as far as you need to go for now. You and your lender can decide on the exact interest rate later when you hammer out the terms of your agreement. Or your lender might propose an adjustable interest rate for a long-term loan.

When and How Do You Want to Repay?

Although I've been talking up the flexibility of friends and family when it comes to making loans, the bottom line is that most lenders expect to be repaid—and sooner than you might think. In fact, nearly half of private investors expect repayment within two years, and almost three-quarters expect to be repaid within five years. In preparation for approaching your lender, you'll need to design a repayment plan that covers:

- **payment frequency**—how often you'll make payments
- **alternatives to scheduling identical monthly payments**—whether all your payments will be of the same amount and at the same time, or whether you'll choose an alternate arrangement with variable payment rates or times
- **payment amount**—how much you'll pay per installment, and
- **payment logistics**—whether you or a hired third party will be the one handling the payments and associated paperwork.

Keeping Interest Payments in the Family

Dale needed three new trucks for his fast-growing kitchen remodeling business. He found a dealer with the trucks he wanted, at the price he wanted. Based on Dale's established business, solid revenue, and good credit, the dealer's financing program offered him a rate of 7.2% for a $66,000 loan, to be secured by the new trucks.

Dale could afford the loan—7.2% wasn't at all unreasonable. But he got to thinking about how much he would pay the company in interest on top of the price tag for the three new trucks and wondered whether there were any alternatives.

A few days later, Dale visited his mother, who happened to mention that her CD investments were earning barely 4%. She asked whether Dale knew of any investments that would be secure but would earn her a higher return.

That night, Dale drew up two loan request letters, one to his mother and one to his grandmother (Dale knew that she, too, had a considerable portion of her retirement assets in low-interest CDs). Dale prepared the requests so that they offered the same terms as the dealer-financing program had offered him: 7.2% interest for a secured loan of $33,000. Dale's main goal was to make the loans safe. He felt confident with the course his business was taking, and in case of problems, his family would gain the right to sell his trucks.

Dale's mother and grandmother were both delighted by his offer. He also told each up front that he'd already been approved for financing at the same rate by the dealer, so that they wouldn't feel under any pressure to say yes—he had, after all, other options. Dale offered to retain a loan servicing company, "so we wouldn't have to talk about the loans over the supper table."

Both loans are currently in active repayment. "There's just no sense in paying 7.2% to the dealer when I could be paying it to my family," Dale notes.

TIP

You don't need to write up your repayment plan yet. For now, simply consider your options and take notes for your own use. Later, after you've begun discussions with your prospective lender, you'll look back at these notes, make adjustments according to your discussions, and then write up a more formal plan that meets both your needs. You'll include this as part of your promissory note (the focus of Chapter 9, which includes a section on "Creating Your Repayment Schedule").

Payment Frequency

You can schedule your loan payments to come due monthly, quarterly, semiannually (twice a year), or annually. Or, if you and your lender prefer not to deal with a long string of small payments, you can simply agree that you'll repay the entire amount (with interest) as a lump sum on a certain date.

I recommend you stick with a traditional monthly loan commitment. Monthly payments are habit-forming—the good kind of habit. By forcing yourself to start making monthly payments as soon as possible, you will build your lender's confidence in you, develop financial practices that will be crucial to your success, and may even boost your credit score.

TIP

What if you're pretty sure you won't be able to make your payments right away? You can structure your loan agreement to account for this, for example, by commencing your repayment schedule after a few months or quarters or by starting out making interest-only payments. After the start-up phase, your agreement should shift into a regular repayment schedule.

Alternatives to Scheduling Identical Monthly Payments

The standard, easy way to pay back a loan is for every payment to include the same amount of principal and interest, and for payments to be made on a regular schedule, month by month or period by period. (This is called an "amortized loan.") However, as the field of financing has become more sophisticated, a number of new options have opened up. The ones you're most likely to find useful include not only the traditional amortized loan, but also those called "graduated," "interest-only," and "seasonal" loans.

You might also make your life easier by adding special provisions to your agreement allowing for deferred payments and a grace period for your regular payments. To determine how much each payment will be, you'll need to use a loan calculator (described in "How to Figure Out Your Payment Amount" below).

Amortized Loan

Let's start with the easy case, a perfectly viable choice. In an amortized loan, each payment consists of a combination of principal (the actual amount you owe) and interest (the extra amount you pay for use of the lender's money). You've probably dealt with an amortized repayment schedule before, when paying off a car loan or a mortgage. You must pay the exact same amount in monthly or other periodic installments over the term of the loan, illustrated in the graphic below. You should select an amortized repayment plan only if you're reasonably certain you'll have an adequate cash flow from early on, as well as consistently throughout your business cycle.

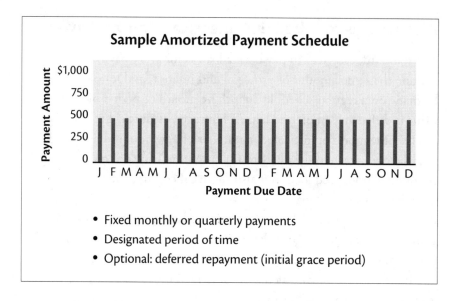

Sample Amortized Payment Schedule

- Fixed monthly or quarterly payments
- Designated period of time
- Optional: deferred repayment (initial grace period)

Graduated or Start-Up Loan

Similar to an amortized loan, a graduated loan would require you to make regular payments consisting of a combination of principal and interest. However, the amount you'd pay each time would vary, as you can see in the sample below. You'd start off making reasonably low payments and later increase these by a scheduled percentage, before leveling off to a fixed amount for the remaining loan term. These increases are called "steps," and loan calculators allow you to select how many steps you will have in your graduated loan. This is an excellent repayment choice for most new businesses that need time to get up and running. Loan calculators can also help you consider how your payments on a graduated loan would change over time.

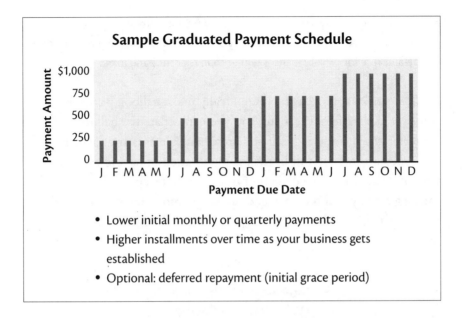

Sample Graduated Payment Schedule

- Lower initial monthly or quarterly payments
- Higher installments over time as your business gets established
- Optional: deferred repayment (initial grace period)

Interest-Only Loan

As the name suggests, an interest-only loan allows you to make payments of pure interest over a number of months or years. Most interest-only loans end with a final payment that includes the last bit of interest owed plus the entire amount of the principal (called a "balloon payment"). The sample below shows how the numbers play out. On the one hand, this plan keeps your monthly payments very low. On the other hand, by not repaying any of the principal along the way, you will find yourself well into the loan without having reduced the total amount you owe by even a penny. And unless you are well prepared, the balloon payment can be very difficult to make.

TIP

Balloon payments can blow up on you. Putting off making a large, lump sum payment until the end of your loan term carries obvious risks. What if your business hasn't gone well, or for other reasons you haven't saved enough to basically repay the entire loan at once? By now, your lender's enthusiasm for your business idea may have faded, and he or she may be reluctant to renegotiate the loan. Unfortunately, you wouldn't be the first entrepreneur to regret having entered into this tempting loan arrangement—it's one of the main reasons that the default rate for private loans is higher than that for bank loans.

A less risky approach is to periodically make balloon payments throughout the life of the loan. And you can deflate the balloon payment by remembering that you aren't stuck in this arrangement—if you someday find yourself in the happy situation of having extra cash, you can usually prepay portions of or the entire principal. But over the long term, you'll probably end up paying more interest than with an amortized loan. That's because you're taking longer to pay off the principal.

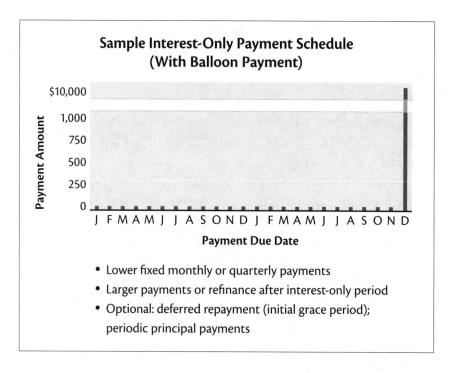

Sample Interest-Only Payment Schedule (With Balloon Payment)

- Lower fixed monthly or quarterly payments
- Larger payments or refinance after interest-only period
- Optional: deferred repayment (initial grace period); periodic principal payments

Seasonal

Some businesses live and die with the seasons, meaning that they earn significant revenue only during certain months of the year. Usually, tourism- and holiday-related businesses have considerable fluctuations in their annual cash flow. For example, although Mack & Manco's Pizza on the Ocean City boardwalk in New Jersey is a year-round business, its pizza sales soar in June, July, and August when all the visitors come to town. If your business is seasonal, you might consider a repayment plan that allows you to make lower payments during the off-season months and higher payments during the high-season months, as illustrated in the sample schedule below.

One of CircleLending's earliest clients was a thriving Halloween products business. Despite its success, August, September, and October were the only months during which it drew in any significant revenue. On top of this concern, the business needed cash early in the year, in order to make purchases from overseas suppliers. To accommodate these unusual needs, the owner and his lender customized a payment plan allowing the owner to make interest-only payments in the off-season months, and larger payments, which included a portion of the principal, during the Halloween-season months. I've never heard of a bank extending this kind of repayment plan.

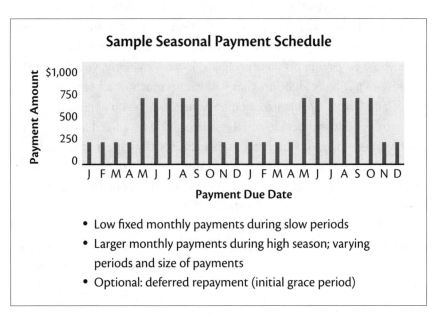

Sample Seasonal Payment Schedule

- Low fixed monthly payments during slow periods
- Larger monthly payments during high season; varying periods and size of payments
- Optional: deferred repayment (initial grace period)

TIP

You can design a one-of-a-kind repayment plan. While the repayment plan types described above are the easiest and most commonly used, you're not limited to these. I've known creative entrepreneurs who combined two or more of the standard repayment plans to fit the expected cash flow of the business at different points over the life of the loan. It's all up to your ability to anticipate your needs and your lender's willingness to be flexible. For example, one way for borrowers to convince lenders to accept a lower interest rate is to provide them a bonus payment in the event the business does well. A bonus payment of $10,000 if your business succeeds in getting a key contract might be enough to convince your lender to accept a low-interest loan with a long grace period.

How to Figure Out Your Payment Amount

One of the first questions I ask someone who's entering into a friends-or-family loan is, "How much can you afford to pay each period?" (whether monthly, quarterly, or on some alternate schedule). Before you answer this question, look at the financial projections in your business plan—in particular, at the cash flow you've predicted during the months or years you'll be paying off your proposed loan. Obviously, you shouldn't promise to pay back amounts that will eat up much or all of your projected income. Determine a range of how much you can afford to pay each period, and decide whether that should be a fixed amount over the life of the loan, or whether you can realistically expect to increase your payments after your business gets underway. Plan carefully for a repayment schedule where your payments will always be less than your income projections.

How much you'll pay per installment is a simple matter of mathematical calculation, after you've determined the total loan amount, the interest rate, the term of the loan—that is, the length of time until it's paid off, typically three to five years—and the schedule or type of repayment plan. Loan calculators will help you do the math. Simply enter the appropriate information for the type of loan you're considering—such as the loan amount, the annual interest rate, the term (number of months) of the loan, and payment frequency—and the calculator will generate a schedule of payments.

 RESOURCE

Where to find loan calculators. You can find loan calculators many places online, including:

- Nolo, www.nolo.com (check the calculators in the Legal Encyclopedia)
- Yahoo, http://smallbusiness.yahoo.com/r-calculator-loan, and
- Bankrate.com, www.bankrate.com/calculators.aspx.

With a loan calculator, you can try a variety of combinations until you find a payment schedule that works for you. If the term of the loan and the interest rate you imagined leave you with monthly payments that aren't affordable for your business, try a longer term or a lower interest rate.

Let's follow the thinking and calculation process used by Bill (whom you read about in "Even Family Might Require Collateral," above), when he borrowed $20,000 from his father to start Neighborhood Transmission Services. In planning his repayment schedule, Bill used a loan calculator to compare two options: amortized and interest-only loans.

First, Bill plugged in the terms for an amortized loan at 8% interest, which he found would require him to make quarterly payments of $2,730 for two years, for a total interest payment of $1,842. Bill kept a copy of that table:

Amortized Payment Schedule

$20,000 loan, 8% interest, quarterly payments for two years

Due date	Principal	Interest	Total
11/1/2009	$2,330.20	$400.00	$2,730.20
2/1/2010	2,376.80	353.40	2,730.20
5/1/2010	2,424.34	305.86	2,730.20
8/1/2010	2,472.83	257.37	2,730.20
11/1/2010	2,522.28	207.92	2,730.20
2/1/2011	2,572.73	157.47	2,730.20
5/1/2011	2,624.18	106.02	2,730.20
8/1/2011	2,676.64	53.53	2,730.17
Total:	$20,000.00	$1,841.57	$21,841.57

Then, Bill plugged in the same terms but changed one, the payment schedule, to make it an interest-only loan (see below). Bill was stunned to see that, although he'd have payments of only $400 each quarter, overall they'd add up to $3,200 in interest—for the same-sized loan! Plus, on one day two years from the start date, he'd get slammed with a $20,400 payment. That was a day Bill decided he'd avoid entirely—he went with the amortized loan.

Interest-Only Payment Schedule

$20,000 loan, 8% interest, quarterly payments for two years

Due date	Principal	Interest	Total
11/1/2009	$0.00	$400.00	$400.00
2/1/2010	0.00	400.00	400.00
5/1/2010	0.00	400.00	400.00
8/1/2010	0.00	400.00	400.00
11/1/2010	0.00	400.00	400.00
2/1/2011	0.00	400.00	400.00
5/1/2011	0.00	400.00	400.00
8/1/2011	20,000.00	400.00	20,400.00
Total:	$20,000.00	$3,200.00	$23,200.00

> **RESOURCE**
> "Creating Your Repayment Schedule" in Chapter 9 includes
> repayment schedules for these and other types of loans, including loans with
> seasonal and graduated payments.

What Are Your Options as to Payment Logistics?

The final thing to consider is what you'll tell your lender about the logistics of repayment—literally, who will take care of sending your checks on time. Whomever you choose will also need to deal appropriately with any late or missed payments. In addition, your business will need to file end-of-year reporting and tax statements for your lender's (or your lender's accountant's) use in preparing his or her own tax returns. You have two main options for who handles all this.

Do It Yourself

You can send a check every period by the due date specified in your promissory note. If you choose this route, you'll also need to keep a loan log (see how to do so in Chapter 10), and will probably want to hire an accountant to prepare a year-end report of the loan for the lender's taxes (and for yourself, if you have a profitable business and are deducting the interest from profits).

The benefit of handling repayment yourself is that it keeps the relationship informal and costs less out of pocket. The challenge is that it's one more piece of paperwork you need to worry about and spend your valuable time on. Additionally, both you and your lender may actually prefer that the relationship be a formal one, handled by someone else. If you think this is the case, consider the next option.

Hire a Neutral Third Party to Manage Repayment

Consider hiring an accountant, financial adviser, attorney, or other third party to manage your private loan. The benefit is that this makes the relationship more formal, like a business transaction, not a personal contact. It creates a buffer so that if there is a problem, someone else will sort it out and you and your lender will hardly need to discuss it.

You can expect to pay $100 to $150 per hour to hire an accountant to administer your loan. It may take no more than an hour per month to administer (including reminding you to pay, receiving the payment and depositing it into your lender's account, and following up for late or missing payments). On the other hand, if you're making monthly payments, this bill can add up. In addition, your accountant will need to provide an end-of-the-year tax report to both you and your lender, which may take one to three hours to prepare. If there are any complications in the records, like a few missed payments or changes in the payment schedule, or if the person creating the report is different from the one managing payments, preparation of year-end reports can certainly take longer.

If you were to hire a loan servicing company, you'd typically pay a setup fee for documents unique to your state and situation, then a small monthly fee for ongoing service, including year-end tax reporting and credit reporting, if needed.

CHAPTER

7

Drafting a Loan Request Letter

FORMS ON CD-ROM

Chapter 7 includes instructions for, and a sample of, the following form, which is in Appendix B and on the Loan Forms CD included at the back of this book:

- Loan Request Letter

Once you've made some basic decisions as to the interest rate and other loan terms you want to offer potential lenders, the next step is to collect your thoughts into a draft loan request letter. Don't send the letter yet—we're still in the realm of background work. As you'll see in Chapter 8, it's best to make personal contact with your prospect first, to talk about your idea. But as soon as your prospect either invites you to send some information or actually agrees verbally to the idea of a loan, you'll want to have your draft letter all but ready to send.

Unlike the lengthy loan applications that banks and institutional lenders demand, loan request letters to friend and family lenders have no standard format or required elements. Most can take the form of a one- or two-page letter from you to your potential lender.

The sample letter outlined here is just that: a sample. Don't use it word for word, but do feel free to adapt it to your needs. If you use it more than once, adapt it each time so each prospect receives a personalized request. (Family members, in particular, are likely to compare letters.) By the time your prospect finishes reading this letter, he or she should know that you are asking for a loan for your business, how much money you need, what interest rate you are offering, and when to expect repayment.

What to Include in a Loan Request Letter

Here are the basic elements to include in a loan request letter:

- **An opening.** State your purpose for writing, namely to raise a stated amount of money for a particular business. Specify the amount or the range you're asking of this prospect.
- **A progress report.** Mention how much money you've already raised, if relevant. This helps the lender understand that you're serious, and that other people are convinced that your business is worth lending money to.
- **Description of the business, service, or product.** Describe what you do (or plan to do), the need it fills, and the expected market for it.

- **Description of who will manage the business.** Say why you and any cofounders are well suited to running this business, including your relevant skills and experience.
- **Summary of your proposed loan terms.** Draw on the background work and loan calculations you did in Chapter 6 to summarize the loan terms you're offering. You can either do this right in the letter or attach additional sheets summarizing the loan options.
- **Your loan servicing plan.** Indicate how you propose to set up and handle loan payments and related paperwork, and whether or not an outside agency or person is involved.
- **A respectful and enthusiastic closing.** This is a personal letter, not a legal document. Sign off in a way that reminds the person of any previous conversations you've had and sets the stage for future conversations.

The sample loan proposal letter for Esme's Cafe shown below is an actual letter I created for a client, whom I'll call Esmeralda. At the time we drafted this letter, Esme (her nickname) needed $15,000 to open her downtown bakery and had already raised $10,000. She'd decided to offer anywhere from 10% to 15% interest to entice her prospects, but was still unsure of which combination of amounts and interest rates would move people to sign on the dotted line. The two prospects she'd already contacted about her business idea were colleagues of an acquaintance, so they were fairly distant to her, but both were successful women known for their private support of female entrepreneurs throughout the city. Both women had, over the phone, invited Esme to send more materials for their consideration.

Esme polished up her business plan with a local business counselor. After that, the two of us designed a menu of three loan options from which her savvy and analytical lenders could choose. All three were for an amortized two-year loan with an initial six-month deferment period. However, the amounts and interest rates were different. The prospect could choose between making a loan of $2,500 at an interest rate of 10%; $3,000 at an interest rate of 12%; or $5,000 at an interest rate of 15%.

Sample Loan Proposal Letter: Esme's Cafe

Dear Friend and Supporter,

(1) I am excited to tell you about a way for you to support Esme's Café and earn an attractive return. Esme's Café is raising $15,000 from relatives, friends, and business associates, and I thought you might be interested in participating. Attached to this letter are three loan options for you to consider; the loan amount and interest rate vary with each.

(2) I've already raised $10,000 from family members and from a first-place award in a local business plan competition. I thought you might be interested in providing a loan for the remaining $5,000.

(3) Esme's Café is located at the heart of a thriving residential and business neighborhood, close to high-profile city landmarks like the train station and the university. Esme's Café will tap into this bustling market by providing specialty coffee, baked goods, wrapped sandwiches, and cold drinks. In addition to the high visibility and foot traffic of the location, two new government offices across the street employ together about 1,800 people, ensuring a steady stream of customers.

(4) Based on my 20+ years of experience in the restaurant industry and in sales and marketing in our area, I truly believe that this café in this location is a winning combination. In case you are interested in additional business and financial information, I have also included my business plan for your review.

(5) I offer you this opportunity because I believe it is good for my business and good for you. For me, it allows me to raise the money I need to grow my business from people I trust, and at an affordable rate. For you, the 10%, 12%, and 15% interest rates I'm offering provide a competitive short-term return on your money. If you choose to make the loan, after a six-month grace period, you will receive monthly installments for 18 months.

Sample Loan Proposal Letter: Esme's Cafe (continued)

(6) In addition, my proposal offers you the protection of a legally binding loan agreement and the convenience of a third party to manage the repayment. I have retained a firm that specializes in the administration of private loans between relatives, friends, and business associates to handle our loan. We have created a promissory note for—and the firm will manage the repayment of—the loan. My repayments to you will be preauthorized to come out of the Esme's Café corporate account electronically, and the funds will be deposited into a bank account that you designate. We will also provide real-time access (both online and toll free) to payment status and history, maintain records, and provide year-end tax summary reports.

(7) I hope that you will consider this mutually beneficial opportunity. I truly believe that Esme's Café is poised for success and I look forward to your support in growing the business. Thank you for your consideration; I look forward to discussing this opportunity with you further.

Sincerely,

Esmerelda Sanchez

Esmerelda Sanchez
Esme's Cafe

Using the Sample Loan Request Letter as Your Guide

Let me point out some features of Esme's letter that you might choose to adapt for your own use, or change entirely. (The basic letter is included in Appendix B and on the Loan Forms CD accompanying this book.)

1 Remember, Esme had only spoken with her prospects by phone; she'd never actually met them. When we drafted the letter, we made it somewhat formal, to reflect both the distance in the relationship and the fact that both prospects were savvy and analytical. However, if you're preparing your letter for a prospect with whom you have an informal, friendly relationship, you'll want to make the tone a bit less formal. Just don't go too far. Even the closest family and friends feel most confident when their private business loan is treated as a business deal instead of an off-the-cuff favor.

You'll also notice that this borrower chose to give the reader various loan amount options, for the business reasons described earlier. Of course, you don't have to offer your lender such options—you can just state in this opening section how much you're asking of this particular lender, or state a range of loan amounts and leave it at that.

2 Notice that the letter mentions funds that had already been raised. If you can do the same, such information will greatly boost the credibility of your loan proposal. The psychology is simple: "If so-and-so thinks this is a sound business idea, why shouldn't I participate, too?" If you use this approach, be sure to say exactly how much you've already raised towards your goal and how much remains.

3 Fortunately, Esme had already prepared a solid business plan, from which it was easy to glean information about the business, the product, the opportunity, and the market. Beyond the basics, don't spend too much time on business details. The purpose of the proposal letter is not to sell your business—but to sell the idea of a loan to your business. If the prospect wants more information about the business, you'll be able to attach a copy of your executive summary or your full business plan (which is just what we did).

4 It's always important to announce why you are the right person for the job, even if your background is far different from the one described in this sample. No matter what, try to communicate your unique passion and expertise. If you have cofounders, certainly identify them, and if one or more brings something compelling to the business, state it. Be brief, though; this is not the place to sketch out your current or dream organizational chart.

5 In spelling out more of the terms of the loan request, notice that we opened with a statement about how a private loan is mutually beneficial. Although some lenders are in it for the money, many are also in it to help you out, and it's smart to recognize that intention in your letter. If you don't attach options as separate sheets, or if you want to offer only one, you could adapt the paragraph like this:

> For you, the 10% interest rate I'm offering provides a competitive short-term return on your money. If you choose to make a $5,000 loan, after a six-month grace period you will receive monthly installments of $238 for 24 months, resulting in a total repayment of $5,724.

6 Obviously, because I drafted this sample for a client wishing to use a loan servicing company, the letter refers to one. If you'll be handling repayment on your own, however, you could say something like the following:

> In addition, my proposal offers you the protection of a legally binding loan agreement. If you agree to the loan terms set forth in this letter, I'll prepare a promissory note reflecting my promise to repay the loan at these terms. The loan will start on the day we transfer the funds, and monthly payments will begin six months later, on the first of each month. I'll send a check from my business account to the address you specify, will maintain a loan log of my payments, and will have my accountant provide you year-end tax summary reports.

⑦ The formality of your closing will depend a great deal on your relationship with your lender. This letter takes a businesslike tone because it was to be used with acquaintances, not family members. Your own letter might sound much more conversational—for example, you might say, "I hope that you've gotten a better idea of my plans by seeing them in writing. Of course, we'll want to talk this over more in person, perhaps after next week's picnic."

What's Next?

Once you've drafted a loan request letter, you're ready to make your "kitchen table pitch," and then do a final version of the loan request letter that's tailored to your individual lender's personality and needs. Chapter 8 provides advice on doing this (see "After Your Prospect Says 'Yes' (or 'Maybe')").

Making the "Kitchen Table Pitch"

Actually asking for the loan is, for many entrepreneurs, the most fear-inducing part of this process. My job in this chapter is to help you ask in a way that feels natural to both you and your prospect. To do so, you'll want to prepare what I call the "kitchen table pitch."

You may have heard of the "elevator pitch" entrepreneurs use when raising money from venture capital investors. They script and practice a slick sales pitch for use when they have a potential investor cornered and only one to three minutes to make a lasting impression. Your friends, family, and others probably don't want to hear a slick sales pitch, but they certainly do want to look you in the eye and hear a straightforward account of your plans. In contrast to the anonymous and often aggressive approach embodied in the elevator pitch, your approach should be warm, informal, and in keeping with the relationship that you've already built with the person. At the same time, a "pitch" is, by nature, short and snappy.

This chapter will show you how to make a kitchen table pitch—specifically, how to:

- plan where and how you'll make your pitch, and what to bring along
- make a compelling pitch
- handle hesitancy and concerns
- follow up (with the loan request letter you drafted in Chapter 7) after the prospect says "yes" or "maybe," and
- follow up if your prospect says "no."

Planning How You'll Approach Your Prospective Lender

Asking for money may not be as big a deal as you might imagine. Your friends and family won't gasp or faint at your suggestion—they're more likely to be intrigued by your business plans or even flattered that you've thought to involve them.

Some people may actually jump at your request. Remember our example of Dale (see "Keeping Interest Payments in the Family" in Chapter 6), who offered his mother and grandmother a loan arrangement at an interest rate that was nearly double what they were earning on their CD investments? They couldn't wait to invest—the decision was an obvious and easy one. But make no mistake; they wouldn't have been half as eager if Dale hadn't done his homework. He'd researched his and his lenders' alternatives and had made the investment safe by securing the loan and setting up a repayment plan he could easily meet. He was able to offer the loan as a win–win situation so that, according to Dale, the actual asking wasn't hard at all.

Every private loan request will be different, and there's no predicting how yours will unfold. But especially if you don't have an offer that's as cut and dried as Dale's, you'll do best by planning the actual request in advance, backed up by a solid business plan. Here's what works:

1. Decide whether it's better to bring your request up in casual conversation or at an informal meeting.
2. Pick a setting that's suited to your relationship.
3. If you'll be holding a meeting, bring a few well-chosen illustrative materials.
4. Consider email or a phone call to introduce the idea gently, and only follow up with a request if it's invited.

Casual Conversation or Informal Meeting?

The first decision is just how casual you should make your first approach. For some people, it might be appropriate to bring up the request in an email or casual conversation, while for others, you'll be better off scheduling an informal meeting.

If your prospect is someone you see regularly in settings where you have the time and privacy to chat about your personal and professional life, then bringing up your request in casual conversation is probably the right choice. Most entrepreneurs requesting private loans from family members do so during a discussion about what's going on in their life, something family members naturally want to hear about.

If you decide to ask for money in casual conversation, the idea is to let it come up when the conversation turns to you and your work. Instead of directly asking the listener for money, you'll phrase it more generally, saying that you need to raise some money for your business and you're trying to figure out how to do it and whom to ask. You'll learn more about this gentle approach in "Easing Into Your Request," below. People like to be asked for advice, and that can often lead to financial support.

If you're asking for money from someone whom you don't see every day, or for whom a more business-like setting seems appropriate, then you're better off scheduling an actual meeting. Call or email the person and say that you would like to get his or her input on your business idea, then set a time and place to meet. There's no need to deceive your prospect about the purpose of the meeting, but you also don't want the meeting to sound like a sales pitch before it even starts. Keep your meeting request friendly and show your genuine excitement at sharing your business idea and hearing the other person's thoughts.

One person I approached when raising money for CircleLending was a long-time friend from high school who was married to an investment banker. The couple had made some other informal investments. I set up a meeting over a weekend lunch, after explaining that I needed their advice. After some genuine small talk, I started to tell them about my business idea and asked for guidance on fundraising. Soon they were on my side, brainstorming people whom I should contact. Before they knew it, they were suggesting making an investment to help me get started.

Where's the Best Place to Meet?

An actual kitchen table is, of course, not crucial to your kitchen table pitch. However, whether you elect to schedule a meeting in advance or not, you should choose a setting that is similarly comfortable and informal. The closer the relationship, the more informal the setting should ordinarily be. For example, when I first approached my aunt about a business loan, I opted for a "home theater pitch"—in the basement of her home, where our families had watched many movies together. There was no need to schedule this one ahead of time: I simply brought up the topic of my new business on one of my regular visits, when we were discussing family news.

The more distant the relationship, the more formal the setting might be—for example, at the person's office, a restaurant, or on other neutral ground. When I was ready to raise money from some business associates, I sent an email inviting them to join me over lunch in a conference room we used regularly for business meetings. I billed it as a brainstorming meeting for my new business concept, and they were eager to give me their ideas. Though a conference room may sound somewhat formal, it put us all at ease because we had spent much time together there. We all felt like we were in our "comfort zone" in those swivel chairs overlooking the Charles River.

A restaurant or café is a good location for meeting someone with whom you're not especially close. It's a common location for mixing business and pleasure, and one where neither of you enjoys a home turf advantage. With the waitstaff taking care of details like refilling the coffee cups, you're free to concentrate on your conversation. And most towns offer a wide variety of restaurants, so that you can find a cuisine and ambience that both of you will enjoy.

However, restaurants have some disadvantages as meeting places, too. The main one is that someone has to pay the bill—and there's no obvious answer as to who should do so. If you pick up the tab, the potential lender may feel that you're too loose with money or don't need his or her help. If you don't pay the bill, the lender may feel insulted—here you've gone and suggested the meeting, asked for money, and now you want to be treated to a free meal as well? There's no way to know which reaction you'll get. Some entrepreneurs go so far as to say that you should never meet at restaurants at all.

I suggest a more moderate approach: If you feel that a restaurant setting suits you and your potential lender, choose an inexpensive restaurant (preferably one that's a cut above a greasy spoon or fast food) and pick up the tab. That way you can assume the role of host and prove your thriftiness all at once.

TIP
Are you on a strictly fast-food budget? If so, opt for a meeting in an upscale coffee house instead of a fast-food chain restaurant. A gourmet cup of coffee makes a better business impression than a burger and fries served at a plastic table.

In the end, your instincts will be the best guide to a location that will put your potential lender at ease and in good spirits. Draw on your past together and your relationship to think up the right place.

What Can You Bring to Illustrate Your Plans?

Your casual conversation is not the time to bring along notebooks full of business plans and promissory notes—particularly if you plan to "just happen" to run into your relative while he or she is walking the dog. But if you decide to use an informal meeting to first bring up your request, bring something tangible to show the person. A brochure, a sample product, a website, or an article in the newspaper would all serve to explain your business and give it credibility. Pick something you can slip into your purse, pocket, or backpack and that doesn't require a carrying case or overhead projector.

Also make sure that whatever you bring makes your idea come to life. Photos or drawings of your product or planned site are particularly good, since visuals attract people's attention and take your description out of the realm of the imagination. If you plan to open a bakery, bring sample cookies. If you have your laptop with you or a cell phone with Internet access, your newly launched website can be effective for show and tell.

If you don't have any such materials on hand, it's okay to create something just for the meeting. Even something as simple as a printout of a color logo and tagline can help others get a more tangible sense of your business idea.

At one of my informal meetings in a shared conference room, I was surprised at how much my prospects liked some presentation boards I assembled. They contained graphics describing my first product, called

Brochure for Fictional Coat Designer

Concetta Coats

Winter will be your favorite season

Handshake Plus, a private loan setup and management service. I paid a graphic designer for a few hours of work to design the boards, which included my business logo, bullet point highlights of the product (how it would work, the price), and a picture I'd found on the Web of two people shaking hands.

> **TIP**
>
> **A business logo always makes a good impression.** Try to have yours ready for any important lender meeting, especially if you're talking about a sizable loan. Feature your logo on your product brochure or website, a presentation board, or even your business card, and bring these to your informal meeting. If you don't have a logo already, visit www.logoyes.com where, for a reasonable fee, they can help you create one.

Letting the Oven Timer Do the Talking

When Andrea, who is opening a café in Washington, DC, is ready to ask a prospect for money, she invites the person to the café site for the meeting. Often, she plans the visit for a time and a day when at least two things will happen: First, she schedules the delivery van to arrive at that time to pick up the flowers that she arranges and places for several offices weekly (an existing side business that will help support the café in its early stages).

Second, she arranges for the baked goods and coffee that she provides as a catering service (another side business that generates cash for, and word-of-mouth interest in, her café) to be ready. There's nothing better than a timer going off during a meeting indicating that a freshly baked batch of carrot bread or other specialty baked good is ready to be pulled from the oven. One prospect was so pleased by the fresh coffee and carrot bread that he brought his wife back just a few days later to try them for herself. Andrea says, "I like my prospects to see how busy I am; and they are always impressed to see that I'm already in business even though my doors aren't even open."

Making a Compelling Pitch

I can't script your pitch conversation for you—the one where you actually ask for money. Your words and manner will depend on whom you're approaching and how well you know the person. It will also be affected by where you've chosen to approach your prospective lender, and how much they already know about your business. If you've agreed to meet for lunch or coffee, for example, the person will expect a fairly leisurely conversation lasting a good hour or so. The opposite will be true if you plan to simply chat with a family member over the appetizer table at your annual New Year's party.

No matter where you plan to speak with your prospective lender, however, following a few basic principles will give you your best shot at getting an enthusiastic response:

1. Start with your business idea.
2. Ease into the loan request.
3. Keep any agreement verbal.

 TIP

Don't change the way you behave when you ask for money. Be yourself. This even includes dressing like yourself: Showing up in a suit for a restaurant lunch with your mother will probably put her on her guard (unless that's normally how you visit with her).

Creating Excitement Around Your Business Idea

After some small talk, start telling the story of your business plans—whatever part of them you think will most interest your prospective lender. Your job is to spark your prospect's imagination. Describe the great product or service you are developing and why you think it will sell, using any of the materials you've brought along to illustrate your description. (Also, any time that it seems appropriate, you can offer to send a complete copy of your business plan after you get back to your desk.) List several specific business goals you have for the upcoming months, such as trade shows to attend, sales goals to achieve, and new product versions to design. Explain why you think now is the right place and the right time to launch or expand your business—and why you are the right person to do it.

Don't forget, however, that you billed this meeting as a conversation to enlist your prospect's input. Before you've delivered a feature-length monologue about the merits of your idea, ask your prospective lender some genuine questions. Tailor your questions to your prospect's interests or experience—everyone probably knows something relevant to your business, whether from being a fellow business owner, a marketing or communications expert, or simply a choosy consumer. You could ask for ideas on how to make your plan work, or ask what would make this person buy the product or service.

Listen closely to the answers; you may glean useful information, and the answers will give you clues as to where your prospect's true interests lie. The more you leave room for genuine give-and-take, the greater the chances your prospect will suggest participating of his or her own accord.

TIP

Express confidence. Confidence in yourself and in your business idea are critical messages to communicate during this pitch conversation. Of course, that doesn't mean hiding the challenges that you'll face. By showing that you've thought these through and are ready to face up to them, you will only enhance your appearance of readiness. One way to build up some confidence, especially if you don't know your prospective lender very well, is to practice your pitch in advance with a spouse or close friend.

Easing Into Your Request

Many fundraising advisers suggest that you "be direct" in making your request for a loan. Unfortunately, some people take that to mean you should hit lenders with your request before they've even had a chance to open their lunch menu. In my experience with family and friends, it is actually more effective to be comparatively indirect. Yes, you've been waiting a long time and may be eager to just blurt out your question and get it over with. But hold off until you've reached a point in your conversation where the question seems to arise naturally.

Be sure that your prospect is engaged in your idea before you bring up your request for money—that is, if the person hasn't already offered to help. In some cases, you may need only to start talking about what you want to do before your prospect starts volunteering to help make it happen.

> EXAMPLE: When Jay needed $45,000 to launch his general contracting business, he went to a favorite uncle and aunt. The couple already knew he'd been unhappy working for his past employer and planning to start his own company. At a regularly scheduled visit to his uncle and aunt's home, Jay told them he had put together his business plan and was ready to get started. When his aunt asked, "How can we help?" Jay replied that he "needed a lot of money." He asked whether they had any suggestions as to where he should begin looking. To Jay's utter amazement, his uncle asked, "How much is a lot of money?" and proceeded to finance the entire loan.

If you need to make your request more explicitly, use, in the lingo of fundraising, a "soft ask." After some conversation about your business plans, you might say, "I need to raise about X dollars to get started, and I thought you might be interested in participating."

If the person looks at all uncertain at this point, you might acknowledge any tensions that have entered the room with a comment like, "No pressure, of course." Next, explain why you thought of this person; something like, "I thought it might appeal to you because I know you started your own Web design business a few years ago," or "I thought of you because I know you have a background in business." But there's no need to be apologetic or back down—your manner should continue to show your confidence that you've offered your prospect a reasonable investment opportunity.

Cultivating a Prospect Over Several Months

One of Andrea's best loan prospects (for her Washington, DC, café, described earlier) is someone she has never met. The prospect is a friend of a close colleague of Andrea's from her days in hotel food service. When the former colleague heard about Andrea's business plans, he didn't have the money to spare but gave her the number of his friend, a successful doctor.

Andrea didn't know the doctor personally but had seen her at a recent social event. The first time she called, Andrea introduced herself by mentioning the event, using the name of the mutual friend, and saying that her friend indicated the doctor might be looking for local investment opportunities. But Andrea knew it was important to build a relationship with the doctor and spent at least three months building rapport before presenting her actual loan request. This included conversation about Andrea's own heart surgery, the doctor's business dreams, and Andrea's business plans. The doctor, a traveling cardiologist, was rarely in town to meet in person, so all these discussions took place by phone. The doctor even introduced Andrea to an independent coffee supplier, so now her café can carry its own line of coffee beans. Andrea also discovered that this would be the doctor's first private loan and that the doctor hoped to make other loans and one day start her own business.

"The doctor just believes in helping people advance," Andrea notes. Finally Andrea sent the doctor her loan request, packaged with three loan option sheets and a copy of her business plan. The doctor called back, right away, and confirmed, "I want to do it." But that wasn't the end, because the check is not yet in the mail. "I don't want to be pushy," says Andrea, "and I know she means what she says. She's just very hard to pin down."

Wrapping Up the First Conversation

Think of your kitchen table pitch as the mere opening to a longer conversation. Your main goal for the moment is for your prospective lender to say "yes" to the idea of a loan—not to sign on the dotted line. But regardless of whether your prospective lender reacts positively during your pitch, it's best to leave this initial conversation or meeting open-ended. Allow some matters to remain unresolved until after the person has had a chance to think things over. This way, you can keep your potential lender at ease and demonstrate that you, the person the lender knows and trusts, haven't suddenly transformed into an aggressive salesperson.

If the Conversation Goes Well

Let's say the conversation is going well. If you get a "yes," you've crossed into the land of working out the details—details that can just as well be left for later, as discussed below. Explain that you'll send your lender a letter detailing the loan options and next steps. If your lender is nevertheless so gung-ho that he or she can't resist asking a few more questions, there's no need to act coy.

If, for example, your prospect wants to talk about exactly how much you need to borrow, start by offering a range, such as "between $10,000 and $30,000." (The amounts you choose will depend upon the amount you figured out in Chapter 5.) This helps the lender feel like he or she is not rushing into anything and can go home, perhaps contact an accountant, and think about how much he or she can offer.

Repayment is another issue you might touch upon during your conversation but you should try to avoid entangling yourself in deep discussions over. Drawing on your draft loan request letter (which you will soon customize and send to your lender), simply describe how and when you'll pay the money back. For example, you might say, "I'm anticipating a repayment schedule of five years, with interest of course." Most lenders, however, will be glad to have a chance to sit with what they've heard so far and wait to receive your request in writing.

In any case, once your prospect has heard enough to agree to the idea of a loan, it's time to wrap up your pitch conversation. Explain what the next steps will be. Say that you will shortly be sending your business plan and a loan request letter, after which the two of you can hammer out the details of the loan before signing the final agreement. The final step will be what's called the "closing," described at the end of Chapter 9, where you will sign the promissory note and the lender will give you the funds.

I specifically advise against giving the lender a copy of your loan request letter or business plan during this initial conversation or meeting. You should have them virtually ready to send as soon as you get home, but for now, preserve the informality of the meeting and the comfort of the personal relationship by sticking with purely verbal discussions and agreements.

If the Conversation Doesn't Go Well

Now let's imagine that the conversation hasn't gone so swimmingly, and your prospect is uncomfortable or unwilling to agree to a loan. If possible, don't let him or her actually say the word "no." If you sense that the person is trying to find a way to decline, help out by saying something like, "I can tell that you're not comfortable with this yet— can I contact you again in six months to show you my progress?" This lets both of you off the hook for now and gives you a reason to call back six months later (assuming your prospect leaves that door open).

Don't worry; very few people make their financial decisions quickly, let alone on the spot. In fact, entrepreneurs often receive a lukewarm reception long before they get an eventual yes. This is because even your strongest supporters will likely have some questions they need answered before lending you money for your business.

In fact, expect most prospects to go home and review your request and maybe your business plan. Some will want to consult others— probably a spouse or partner, and maybe a professional adviser like an attorney or accountant. It will be up to you to follow up through email, phone, or additional meetings, if these are what the prospect needs to get to yes.

Following Up After Six Months

If you do put your conversation on hold for six months or some other period of time, be sure not to drop the ball after that time has passed (unless it's clearly a no-go or you've raised the money from other sources). One of the most valuable things you can take away from a meeting that didn't go well is an agreement to follow up. This gives you the reason, and the excuse, to call again on this prospect. Even if you choose not to renew your request for a loan, it's only fair to follow up, so that you don't leave the matter hanging between you.

When the agreed-upon period of time has passed, contact the prospect and ask if you can meet again to share the progress your business has made. If the person agrees to a follow-up meeting, that's an excellent sign—it would have been all too easy to just say "no" to your meeting request.

Prepare for the meeting by creating a visual representation of what you achieved in the intervening months. A table, a bar chart, or PowerPoint presentation where you spell out milestones accomplished and those yet to come will be useful. You could even just prepare a checklist of "items accomplished" and "items to do." If you've had any favorable press coverage or customer feedback, those can be very effective at bringing life to your tables and charts.

When you go to the follow-up meeting, bring these materials with you. Your goal is to communicate the progress you've made since you last met. You may even want to make checks on the checklist or use a marker to fill in a bar on a bar chart to illustrate your growth. By showing that you can do what you say you will do, you may cause the person to happily agree to the loan.

Handling Hesitancy and Concerns

Many of the questions you'll hear from prospects will be centered around the loan itself, such as how much money you're asking for, how you'll use the money, when and how you'll repay it, and what happens if you can't repay the loan. You'll already know the answers from having drafted your loan request letter or business plan, and these materials will address many of your prospects' questions.

However, some people may also raise more general concerns, most commonly over their own finances, the viability of your business, the impact on your relationship, and what others might think.

Concerns About the Prospect's Own Financial Limitations

Prospects concerned about their finances may tell you that they don't have the money, it's not handy, or they already have a plan for it. Here are some ways you can respond to their concerns.

"I don't have the money to give you." Suggest a lower amount. Ask whether the person can think of someone else you might contact. Or perhaps the person can help your business in other ways, such as by providing office space, computer equipment, or sales contacts.

"I have other plans for that money." Politely ask about the plans. It may be that you can make the term of your loan short enough to repay your lender in time for the other needs. For example, if a relative has moved children's college savings into a money market account while the kids are still in high school, you could structure your repayment to be completed before college tuition payments begin. In this case, you may want to offer collateral, to offset any risk to the hard-saved education dollars.

"I can't access the money. It's tied up in an investment/retirement plan/ annuity." Encourage your lender to contact his or her financial adviser or accountant to find out whether the money can be moved, without penalty, to an account that allows private investing. For example, a self-directed IRA is a retirement account that allows the account owner to make investments for tax-free retirement investing in private businesses like yours. (See "What to Tell Your Prospect About Self-Directed IRAs," below.)

What to Tell Your Prospect About Self-Directed IRAs

Most folks with IRAs (individual retirement accounts) don't look beyond the standard menu of mutual funds or stocks offered by the financial institution managing the account. They may not realize that a few institutions also allow account holders to invest the money in private business or real estate investment opportunities of the person's own choosing. That gives investors the tax advantages of retirement investing while hand picking their investments.

Only a handful of companies offer a self-directed IRA product, although these are rapidly gaining in popularity. Your prospect should check with a financial adviser about his or her current IRA and whether there are any self-directed IRA products, but chances are he or she will need to set up a new account with one of the few companies that offers them. Two well-known companies are Equity Trust (www.trustetc.com) and Pensco (www.pensco.com); materials about self-directed IRAs are available on both company websites. Suggesting that your lender set up a self-directed IRA to make you a loan may be the type of smart advice that will make your lender consider your proposal from a tax-efficiency point of view.

Concerns About the Viability of Your Business

Your prospect's impression of your business plan will have an inevitable impact on his or her willingness to make the loan. The prospect may be justifiably dubious about how you're going to sell your pet toys or may just be expressing a lack of knowledge about your business or the whole world of business. Remember, you've been living with this idea for months—its brilliance may not be so patently obvious to someone who's hearing it for the first time.

Explaining not only the potential for success, but also the risks associated with a loan to your business, is an important part of your job. Take the time to show why you think you can do what you say you can.

(If you ever make a request to a professional investor for equity capital, you will be put through a particularly painful process called "due diligence," in which the investor sends you pages of questions to answer about how your business works, in addition to doing his or her own analysis of its potential.)

"I don't believe your business will succeed." Offer a loan secured by collateral, if possible, so that the lender will know that, even if your business goes belly up and you don't have a dime, the lender can sell the collateral to cover your debt. Once the prospect believes that the money is safe, you can also explain why you think your business will, in fact, succeed. Send both the executive summary and the complete version of your business plan. Offer to present your plan to your prospect in person and to answer any questions. If you have other lenders or investors, you could ask one to provide a reference.

You can also take steps to show your prospect that you take personal responsibility for the debt—in other words, that he or she will get paid no matter what. If your business is a sole proprietorship, or if you plan to sign the promissory note so the loan is to you instead of to your business, you become personally liable for the debt. If the loan will be to your incorporated business, you can still assume personal liability if you think it would make the difference for your prospect. To do this, add yourself as a coborrower on the promissory note, so that both the business and the individual can be held liable if the loan doesn't get paid. (See Chapter 9 for details on signing promissory notes.)

"I don't think you have the skills to run your business." Emphasize your experience. Talk to your prospect about former jobs you've held that relate to your business. Mention small business training, classes, or workshops you have taken; business counselors you have met with; and people you plan to hire.

If you feel that your responses still don't adequately alleviate the prospect's concerns, and if you respect the person's business experience, take the objections to heart. Ask whether the prospect has any advice for resolving the problems, and heed the advice whether or not you take this person's money.

Concerns About the Impact on Your Relationship

The prospect may naturally be worried about how lending you money will impact his or her relationships, either with you or with others. To reduce the person's sense of relationship risk, reassure him or her that the loan or investment will be kept as businesslike as possible, as follows.

"What if we disagree over the terms of the deal?" Emphasize the flexibility inherent in a private loan like the one you're proposing—there are a multitude of ways to structure the deal, so you're bound to find one that meets both your and your lender's needs. Also explain that the two of you will discuss the terms of your agreement and put them in writing, so that both of you can refer back as needed during the life of the arrangement. Let the prospect know that you're planning on drawing up legally binding agreements and will keep detailed records of payments for accounting and tax purposes. Explain that since this is a private deal, the two of you can always make changes to handle unexpected circumstances. (In fact, loans between family and friends end up being restructured quite often, as we discuss in Chapter 10.)

"I'm afraid that our relationship will suffer if there's a problem paying back the loan." You must respect and acknowledge this fear. Clearly, you don't want your relationship to be damaged, either. Show how you can prevent problems with the loan from turning into problems in the relationship. Point out that the promissory note will include actions to be taken in the case of late payments, missed payments, and default. Also point out that if the two of you decide to use a third party to administer the loan, the third party can advise you on how to handle and resolve problems before they hurt your relationship. Sometimes it helps to know that there will be a buffer between you and your lender.

RELATED TOPICS

For more on this topic, see "Mixing Money and Relationships Can Work," in Chapter 1.

Concerns About What Others May Think

Even if you think your request is only between you and your lender, be aware that the lender may be thinking about what other people will either say about this loan or have said about private lending in general. You can't directly control such external factors, and the opinions or feelings of other people tend to be a common source of lender concern.

Further complicating the picture is that hesitant lenders often point to a third party when they can't bring themselves to say "no" in their own voice. That means they could be expressing real concerns based on outside pressure, or simply using these concerns to mask something that they don't want to tell you. Here are some ways you can respond to such concerns.

"My spouse (or partner) won't like the idea of my lending you the money." Offer to review your loan proposal with your lender's spouse or partner. Reassure your lender that you don't need a decision on the spot—this is a business matter, not a case where you've run out of cash and need a quick handout. Explain how you plan to make it a business transaction by signing a promissory note that obligates you to repay. Or for extra security, offer to provide a secured loan with collateral. (If that's not feasible, your lender's spouse or partner might be comforted by knowing that the promissory note provides solid grounds upon which to sue you if you still don't come through.)

"I have a friend who lent someone money and never got a dime back." Emphasize that if the loan is set up and managed correctly, the likelihood of successful repayment is much higher. Explain what consequences you would face, under the written agreement you plan to sign, if you made a late payment, missed a payment, or defaulted. Also stress why you will be a good borrower—for example, your manic attention to monthly budgets or your track record of paying your credit card bill in full every month. You might even offer to share a copy of your credit report to prove your "loan worthiness." (Copies of your credit report can be obtained once a year for free from a centralized source mandated by the federal government—go to www.annualcreditreport. com, or call 877-322-8228 for more information or to place a request.)

After Your Prospect Says "Yes" (or "Maybe")

Now let's say that your prospect has either verbally agreed to lend you money for your business, or at least promised to think it over after looking at your written loan proposal. Here's where you'll be happy to have done your background work. When you get back to your desk or computer, revisit the loan request you developed in Chapter 7, in order to make additions or changes based on your conversation. Three of the best ways to polish up your written request so as to clinch your lender's interest are to:

- appeal to your lender's personality type
- offer options, including different loan amounts or terms, and
- offer special incentives.

Does the Loan Request Letter Just Seem Wrong for This Lender?

While the one- to two-page loan request letter described in Chapter 7 works well for most lenders, it's not your only option. Here are two other ways to present the information; but you can prepare anything you think will suit your lender.

A slideshow. Some people, especially those with business experience, might respond well to a few PowerPoint slides or a complete slideshow. Especially if you are adept at using charts, graphs, and pictures to tell your story, a slideshow makes a nice focal point for a follow-up meeting.

A concept paper. This is something longer than a letter but shorter than a business plan. You might describe your idea, the need for it, and how it would work. You need not include all the business details like how you're financing the business, how the economics will work, who you intend to do the work, and so on. This presentation works well for supportive lenders who are eager for details but prefer reading a short paper to a complete business plan.

Tailoring Your Loan Request Letter to Your Lender's Personality Type

Depending on your lender's personality, you can vary the loan terms as well as the language in your loan request letter. As you look at your letter, ask yourself: How well does it address this particular potential lender's motives and concerns? Are there subtle ways in which you can alter the proposal itself, or your wording, to make it feel right to the potential lender?

If your lender is savvy. A savvy lender will be attracted to a competitive interest rate, so offer as much as you think you can afford. Websites like www.bankrate.com and others offer interest rate and payment calculators to determine exactly how different interest rates affect your regular payments and total repayment. Your letter might also mention key financial information about your business, such as an impressive growth in revenue or a great profit margin. Be businesslike and succinct in your communications.

If your lender is inexperienced. An inexperienced lender probably agreed to the loan because he or she wants to support you, so it's important to acknowledge the importance of the relationship. But if your lender is inexperienced, it's also your job to make sure he or she understands the risks. Although you don't need to spell out any gruesome worst-case scenarios in your loan request letter, make sure that this person recognizes that if your business doesn't grow the way you plan for it to, you may be at risk of not being able to make your payments and going into default. Even an inexperienced lender should be able to afford to lose the investment. If talk of risk worries your lender, consider securing the loan with collateral or not taking money from this prospect at all.

If your lender is worried. A worried lender needs assurances. Your letter should mention how and when you will pay back the loan, and how you will handle a cash crunch if it occurs. Lenders worried about emotional risk want to feel that the deal is separate from your relationship. If you decide to hire someone else to manage the loan, explain how this approach can keep the lines of separation clear. If you think the lender is also worried about the loan's impact on other friendships or relationships, offer to share the basics of your loan request with the others so that there are no secrets.

If your lender is analytic. An analytic lender wants a hassle-free loan. This means you should have your paperwork in order and make it easy for the lender to be hands-off. In the loan request letter, spell out the details of how the repayment will work. Analytic lenders tend to appreciate the conveniences of loan servicing by third parties, as well as special services such as automatic debiting and crediting of bank accounts. The easier you make it, the better. Also, don't worry this person with a lot of informal communications. There's no need to call and ask details about his or her weekend camping trip if all you need is to ask at which address the lender would like to receive your draft promissory note for review.

Offering Various Loan Options in Your Loan Request Letter

There's no need to give your family and friend lenders a take-it-or-leave-it proposition. You can demonstrate your flexibility by offering several loan options, each containing a different loan amount and interest rate. For example, you might let your prospects choose between a high-interest loan that lasts several years and a shorter-term loan with a lower interest rate. Protect your own interests by suggesting a repayment schedule that suits the unique needs of your business, such as an interest-only loan, a graduated repayment loan, or a seasonal loan.

The sample letter requesting loans for Esme's Café (in Chapter 7) offered three options. (Esmeralda didn't lay these out in the letter, but in a separate attachment; you can format your request either way.) She intentionally matched the higher loan amounts with higher interest rates, in the hopes that a higher rate would motivate a lender to select a larger loan amount. This approach worked, and she actually received a bit more than she needed to launch the café. That allowed her to buy an additional piece of equipment that had been on her radar screen but that she hadn't yet figured how to finance.

Offering Special Incentives

If you feel that your potential lender needs a little extra convincing, you might adjust your proposal to add some special incentives, such as the following.

Offering a Demand Option

If your prospective lender appears to be reluctant only because he or she may need the money back before you're done with it, you can offer to include a "demand option" in your loan agreement. This provision says that at any point during the life of the contract, the lender has the right to demand full repayment. Offering a demand option can be just the tool you'll need to get a hesitant lender on board. Of course, such a provision comes with obvious risks: You need to be prepared for the possibility that the lender could demand payment at any time, and you'll still need to convince your lender that you're capable of repaying the entire loan at a moment's notice. If you want to offer your lender a demand option, but know that you couldn't pay on demand until your business has been up and running for a while, say the first year, one solution might be to offer the demand option but delay the effectiveness of the demand until one year into the term of the note.

Offering an Adjustable Interest Rate

If you're offering any long-term loans—perhaps of three or more years—realize that some of your investors, especially the savvy ones, may be unwilling to let you lock in an interest rate for that length of time. If rates go up, the lender is going to be looking longingly at other investments with higher returns. Of course, no one can predict how far interest rates might rise or fall during the course of your loan. But the savvy investor may want to protect against being stuck with an interest rate that turns out to be on the low side.

To satisfy the lender's interests, you could, for example, structure your loan so that you pay a fixed rate for a year (allowing you to predict your monthly expenses in the early stages of your business), after which the rate becomes adjustable, fluctuating every year. You would probably tie the interest rate to the prime lending rate, perhaps adding a percentage point or two to further attract the lender. This tool may not make a huge difference in your payments but may give the savvy investor some security.

Offering to Make a Bonus Payment

Identify a specific business milestone, such as a level of revenue or a number of customers served. Propose to your lender that, upon reaching that milestone, you'll make a predetermined bonus payment of, for example, $3,000. (This payment would be on top of your regular payments.) Offering such a bonus shows your lender that you are committed to succeeding in your business and helps him or her feel a stake in that success. Of course, it's best to choose milestones that really do reflect success—if, for example, you simply offered a bonus after one year, you'd have no way of predicting your ability to pay it.

SEE AN EXPERT

See an attorney if you want to incorporate elements of an equity investment into your loan agreement. You'll need expert legal advice to create a hybrid that combines the relative safety of a loan with the ownership benefits of an equity investment.

Offering More-Generous Terms to Less-Willing Lenders

If you'll be approaching multiple lenders, try to enter into agreements with your most likely supporters first. These will probably be your closest family members, who may be not only willing, but eager to agree to loans that offer you maximum flexibility at minimum interest. With these loans in hand, you're now free to offer more-secure loan proposals to your less-convinced lenders.

EXAMPLE: Cynthia wants to buy into a health food store franchise but will need $50,000 to do it. She explores several different funding sources, including a bank loan and the franchiser's financing program, but eventually turns to her circle of friends and family.

After presenting her idea, Cynthia receives generous promises of support, in the form of a $20,000 loan from her mother and a $5,000 loan from her sister. They agree to structure each of their loans the same way: with a ten-year term, to start with deferred repayment for one year, turning into an interest-only loan over the following three years (thus keeping Cynthia's payments as low as possible), then becoming a standard amortized loan for the remaining seven years.

However, their offers leave $25,000 to be raised. Cynthia has also identified a number of other prospects, including a distant cousin, a former employer, and an associate from a prior job. Because she has been out of touch which these prospects for a while, she wants to impress them with her professional approach to her private fundraising and to set the stage for a business relationship.

Knowing that her first two loans won't require any payments for a year, Cynthia can approach these prospects with more standard loan offers. Her former boss and associate each end up agreeing to a standard amortized six-year loan beginning after a six-month deferment period. Unfortunately, Cynthia's cousin decides she is not in a position to invest. The terms of all these loans are detailed in "Summary of Loans Obtained by Cynthia for Health Food Store Franchise," below.

Note that, although the various loans in the table are structured very differently, the amount repaid ends up being about the same. With some similarly careful calculating, you can set up loans that feel unique to each lender but that result in monthly payments and an overall total that you can afford.

Summary of Loans Obtained by Cynthia for Health Food Store Franchise

Loan Terms	Mother and Sister	Former Boss and Associate
Loan amount	$25,000	$25,000
Repayment plan	Deferred/Interest-only/Amortized	Amortized
Interest rate	5%	7%
Principal to be repaid	$25,000	$25,000
Interest to be repaid	$3,750 + 4,681.22 = $8,431.22	$6,694.45
Total to be repaid	$33,431.22	$31,694.45
Schedule	One-year grace period; interest-only payment for 3 years ($104.17 each); reverts to amortized loan for 7 years ($353.35 monthly payments)	Six-month grace period; 72 monthly payments of $377.32

CAUTION

Don't forget to calculate your monthly payments under every loan scenario you offer. For example, when Esmeralda offered interest rates of 10%, 12%, and 15%, she accepted the possibility that she might end up paying anywhere between $115, $142, and $242 per loan per month. Make sure the timing and the amount of all the loan repayments are manageable. Consider their impact on your business finances as a whole; don't just consider them one by one. Until the promissory notes are signed, nothing is set in stone. Adjust your requests as your fundraising moves forward to keep your repayment obligations in line with what you can afford.

Dealing With Your Prospects Who Say "No"

What if, even after you try to address your prospective lender's concerns, or the person agrees to review your customized loan request, he or she nevertheless turns you down? Your first task is to listen carefully to the person's reasons. If your prospect expresses concerns that ring true, or if you hear a similar message from several people, you'll learn important lessons for the future. You'll also be able to decide whether to move on, or whether the prospect left some room open for future discussion.

> **CAUTION**
>
> **Don't push so hard that you endanger the underlying personal relationship.** There's no point in arguing with someone who truly doesn't want to loan you money. Some people may not even tell you the real reason for their hesitation. However, for those who openly express a concern that you can allay by providing more information, there's no harm in following up accordingly.

When to Move On

There are two circumstances in which you need to take "no" as the lender's final answer. The first is if your lender has given you a clear and firm refusal and you accept that his or her concerns or objections are valid. Perhaps your proposal is just not a good fit, in which case it's time to focus your fundraising energy elsewhere.

Second, move on if your lender has given you a muddled refusal that seems to be masking some concern that he or she is unwilling to communicate. If some gentle nudging doesn't bring the issue to the surface, you probably want to let sleeping dogs lie. Besides, do you really want to get into a business transaction with someone who won't say what's on his or her mind from the beginning? You'll be much happier dealing with a lender who gives you clear signals and allows you to address real concerns.

When to Ask Again

Just as with your initial pitch, it's worth keeping certain prospects on your list for future contact—especially those who were at least interested enough to review your loan request letter. Keep track of prospects that you sensed had a favorable opinion of you and your business idea but weren't fully convinced for some reason or other. Here are some logical times to return to those people.

When the agreed-upon amount of time has passed since your initial meeting. If your prospect declines for now but welcomes you to call back in six months, do it.

When you've got a more-convincing presentation. As you gain experience in fundraising, you may realize that your early presentation wouldn't have convinced you, either. When you've had more practice and have a more professional proposal to make, contact a reluctant prospect again. However, it's probably wise to let at least a month or two pass, so your prospect doesn't just roll his or her eyes at seeing you back so soon.

When your business has gained a major new customer or supporter. Being able to show that your business model works, and that you are attracting customers and generating revenue, sends a very positive signal to savvy investors. Some lenders and investors don't like to be the first to jump. But if you go back and tell them about the others who have already put their money into the mix, they may want to do the same.

When your potential lender's circumstances have changed. Maybe your prospect has sold some land or stock, received an inheritance, or taken a great new job. And even if your prospect's financial circumstances haven't changed radically, his or her outlook may have changed due to personal circumstances—for example, your prospect may have a new sense of confidence after surviving a difficult divorce and entering a new relationship. Any of these situations might create an opening for you to return with an update on your business progress and a new loan proposal.

Negotiating Final Terms

After you've sent your loan request letter, business plan, and other documentation, you'll probably go back and forth with the lender before you settle on the basic terms of your agreement. Your next step is to put everything in writing with a promissory note, as described in Chapter 9.

Preparing a Promissory Note, Security Agreement, and Other Loan Documents

FORMS ON CD-ROM

Chapter 9 includes instructions for the following forms, which are in Appendix B and on the Loan Forms CD included at the back of this book:

- Promissory Note (for an amortized loan)
- Promissory Note (for a graduated loan)
- Promissory Note (for a seasonal loan)
- Promissory Note (for an interest-only loan)
- Promissory Note Modifications for a Loan to a Business
- Promissory Note Modifications for Signature by Notary Public
- Security Agreement
- UCC Financing Statement

Believe it or not, the hardest part of your work is done. You've asked people for money to grow your business, and some have said yes, they're willing. By now, if all has gone well, you've reached a verbal agreement with your lender(s), customized a loan request letter and sent it to the lender(s), and heard back that each lender is ready to make the loan. Now you just need to document each agreement, receive the actual funds, and formalize the deal(s).

This chapter will help you prepare the primary loan document—the promissory note, including a repayment schedule. It also shows you how prepare a security agreement (if you will be offering collateral for repayment of the loan). But before I get to the actual forms, I want to start by explaining why documentation is so important.

RELATED TOPICS

If you are the lucky recipient of a financial gift for your small business start-up or expansion, see Chapter 11 which covers important documentation you'll need such as a gift letter.

Wal-Mart's Beginnings Included a Loan From Sam Walton's Father-in-Law

The founder of Wal-Mart, Sam Walton, bought his first retail store in 1945 for $25,000 by borrowing $20,000 from his father-in-law, L.S. Robson, and using $5,000 of his own savings. Two-and-a-half years later, Sam repaid his father-in-law. Today, Wal-Mart Stores, Inc., is the world's largest retailer, with around $300 billion in annual sales. (See Sam Walton's biography at http://en.wikipedia.org.)

Why Documentation Is Important

You've heard me talk before about the importance of documentation. But let's give this topic some final attention, lest you be tempted to skip this step and just reach for the check. The most important thing you can do when you receive a private loan is to commit the agreement to writing. Handshakes and oral agreements have been known to work, but they're basically a gamble that everything will go right in the months and years to come—including events outside anyone's control, like a death in the family or change in jobs.

Writing down the loan agreement is just plain smart for the following reasons:

- **It sets expectations.** The simple act of talking through the terms of the deal when the agreement is made ensures that both parties have the same understanding of how it will play out.
- **It puts those expectations into writing.** Having your responsibilities in print and available to both parties also ensures a mutual understanding of how and when your obligation will be met and helps assure your lender that he or she can enforce the promises you've made.
- **It makes the agreement available to others.** Documenting the agreement formalizes it in the eyes of important players in your financial life, such as the IRS, your attorney, your accountant or other professional advisers, or even your family members or those of your lender (particularly important in the event that your lender dies).

How Documentation Sets Expectations

Although the outlines of your agreement may have seemed clear when you shook hands on it, you'll probably be surprised, when walking through the process of formalizing the agreement, at all the unforeseen questions that arise.

Some of the most basic questions include: Is the money a gift? A personal loan? A business loan? Even if you think these issues were covered in your conversation, you may have heard your uncle saying, "I'll put $20,000 into your business" to mean an equity investment, when he meant it as a loan—or vice versa. Either way, the two of you now have conflicting expectations about the nature and timing of repaying the money. If you don't sort out what you each expect will happen next, your relationship will inevitably sour as your uncle waits for repayment to begin while you go about growing your business without a thought to loan payments.

Less-obvious questions about the details of your agreement also need to be dealt with: How will the interest rate be set? What if you don't repay on time? It's no fun going back to someone months later to negotiate such issues. Far better to take the time to talk through the terms and document the agreement at the outset, when everyone is feeling optimistic.

> **EXAMPLE:** Theresa accepts a $20,000 informal loan from her
> aunt and uncle in order to start a computer consulting business.
> They discuss the loan at a family barbecue, where everyone is in
> good spirits, and they decide not to bother signing any formal
> paperwork. A few days later, Theresa's aunt and uncle do their part
> and send her the check. Theresa launches her business and, through
> many long nights of hard work, pushes it to the break-even point
> a year later. She then decides to take her spouse and children on a
> much-needed Disneyland vacation—before repaying a penny of her
> aunt and uncle's loan.
>
> When Theresa's aunt and uncle hear about the vacation, they're
> shocked. They view it as a frivolous expense and can't believe that
> Theresa would have been setting aside vacation money without first
> repaying them. The subsequent family reunion turns into a tense
> affair, with Theresa's aunt and uncle asking pointed questions about
> her airfare and hotel expenses.

If Theresa, in the example above, had simply documented the loan—say, with a promissory note detailing a repayment plan beginning after a 12-month deferment period, maybe with interest accruing during the deferment—her aunt and uncle would not have had any reason to expect repayment yet. Under that agreed-upon schedule, she would not have even missed a payment. In fact, when Theresa's payments began arriving on time, her aunt and uncle might have marveled at her ability to manage the obligations of a new business and a young family at the same time. Instead, both parties had to suffer through hard feelings and misunderstandings—and ultimately draft a promissory note to redeem the situation.

TIP

Private lenders report greater confidence in the borrower when they've signed a promissory note. Even those who started out saying, "C'mon, I trust you; let's not waste time writing this down," often end up glad to have been talked into documenting the transaction. It saves them from any guilty feelings about looking over your shoulder. When the business is going well, they get paid. When the business has hit a rocky spot, the fact that you've missed one of your regularly scheduled payments means that they're among the first to know.

Why You Want These Expectations in Writing

With everything you have to deal with in running your business, the last thing you need is a cloud of unclear or shifting expectations hanging over your head. Each month when you do the books, you'll be plenty clear on how much you owe to your landlord, your suppliers, and your advertisers. But what about your mother? If she gave you $8,000 to get started, would you know or remember exactly when and how she wanted it back? Having a written document to refer to is the cleanest way to run your business.

Your lender will also appreciate the legally binding nature of a written agreement. Part of your job in persuading someone to make a loan is assuring the person that he or she will have recourse beyond just chasing you down to fulfill your half of the deal. That recourse may include going to court. Courts are far more easily persuaded by signed documents than by oral so-called promises. And if it ever comes to a court battle, you, too, will probably appreciate that the judge won't be choosing between your word and the lender's. (Fortunately, lawsuits rarely happen in private financing situations.)

A promissory note is the main document you need to prepare for a loan. For gifts, you'll need a letter from the person who made the gift (the subject of Chapter 11).

TIP

Written agreements create a framework, not a cage. While your promissory note makes your debt to your lender binding, the way in which you repay the debt can be adjusted along the way to accommodate changing circumstances. Neither you nor your lender need worry that you'll feel constrained by the agreement—but you'll probably be happy to have it as a starting point.

Perhaps more than any other type of cash injection, loans can give rise to all manner of later misunderstandings if undocumented or poorly documented. For example, a loan with a monthly repayment plan gives you twelve times a year when something can go wrong—maybe because you didn't pay, didn't pay enough, paid late, and so on. But a promissory note will include repayment terms which state exactly how much is due and on what dates. If you can't make a payment, the plan itself will tell you how to proceed.

How Documentation Helps With Taxes, Estate Planning, and Other Legal Issues

You and your lenders aren't the only people who might take an interest in your financial agreement. Accountants, attorneys, personal financial advisers, and other professionals may need to see a written contract explaining the terms of the agreement. They, too, need to know what is expected of each party when they review or advise you on your financial situation.

What's more, the documentation may be needed at some point to explain your transaction to the IRS or other oversight agencies. For example, if the IRS or other tax authority were to question whether the arrangement was really a loan, one of its first requests would be for a

What If Your Lender Just Hates Signing Anything?

Even though it's in the lender's best interest to document the loan, family and friends themselves are often the ones to insist that they don't need a bunch of documents to give you money. That can make you feel awkward about turning your supposedly easygoing conversations into a "big deal." But the discomfort you might feel now is nothing compared to the difficulties that might arise later if you don't formalize the loan agreement.

Some lenders aren't merely being polite—they are really, truly uncomfortable about signing formal agreements with a friend or family member. And some people might even feel that it's offensive or inappropriate for you to ask for formal documentation—like you're turning a friendship into a business transaction. If you meet with this level of resistance, try to change your lender's mind—he or she is likely to appreciate it later. You can tactfully try any or all of the following approaches:

- Explain that your accountant needs a legally binding document before you can begin using the money for your business needs.
- Explain that you need to have the documents in place for the IRS, to show that the money is in fact a loan, not a gift.
- Explain that undocumented loans have a higher failure rate and can jeopardize personal relationships.
- Recount a specific case you've heard of where confusion over loan terms and repayment of an undocumented loan ended badly for the borrower and lender. Here's one: When Jay needed capital to build an ice rink, he convinced his dad that the idea would be a success. His dad informally gave him $40,000 over the course of three years. The rink was built but never came anywhere close to turning a profit. Jay had to declare bankruptcy, and his dad turned to his accountant to help write off the bad debt. Unfortunately, there was no loan agreement, and no documentation of any attempts at repayment, and ultimately the IRS wouldn't accept the claim that it was a loss. Not only did Jay's father lose the $40,000 and the chance to write it off, the whole affair created a rift between the father and son that took years to heal.

copy of the promissory note. Or, if you were to default on the loan and be unable to ever repay it, one of the few consolations available to your lender would be a bad debt deduction on his or her taxes. But without a promissory note, the IRS might deny the deduction and call the transfer a gift which has other tax ramifications, as discussed in Chapter 11.

And let's not forget how written documents can avert the family misunderstandings that commonly arise due to undocumented or even poorly documented financing arrangements. For example, let's say you or the person who gave you money dies, leaving behind an outstanding, undocumented gift or loan. During the probate process, the executor of the estate will need proof of the gift or loan in order to allocate money in the proper direction. It's not unusual for other relatives to assume that a money transfer was a loan instead of a gift, especially if they didn't hear about the transfer or didn't receive similar treatment themselves.

> **EXAMPLE:** Serena's grandfather gave her $10,000 one year in order to start a yoga studio. He told her, "No need to repay it; I don't need the money, and I'll get more enjoyment out of watching you fulfill your dreams." Unfortunately, no one overheard this conversation, and the grandfather didn't create a gift letter. He died a few years later. Serena's sisters and brothers got wind of the gift and assumed it to be a loan, since none of them had received a similar gift. If Serena wasn't going to repay it, they wanted to subtract $10,000 from her share of their grandfather's estate. It was Serena's word against theirs. The money was finally treated as a gift, but the conflict left lingering resentments.

ⓘ **TIP**
Documentation is crucial for changing a loan into a gift. Your lender will need to send you what's called a "loan repayment forgiveness letter." Chapter 11 explains how to prepare one and the legal and tax issues involved.

Formalizing a Loan With a Promissory Note

The main legal document you'll need in order to formalize a loan is a promissory note—a written promise to pay the amount you specify, within a period of time you indicate, at a rate of interest you specify. The most basic promissory note could be executed in one sentence—an IOU that could fit on the back of a napkin:

> *Dear Aunt Hilda,*
>
> *I owe you $5,000.*
>
> *Signed, Your Nephew Ben*

However, legal and business realities have stretched the standard promissory note well beyond napkin size. A good promissory note will:
- identify both the borrower and lender by name
- state that the lender has given the borrower sum of money
- set out the repayment terms of the loan, such as the amount per payment and the due dates
- spell out the consequences of late payments, missed payments, and default, and
- contain your (the borrower's) signature.

It's possible to draft your own promissory note without a lawyer, by following the detailed instructions below. If you want to make any major changes, be sure you get the appropriate review (such as by an experienced business or tax attorney).

TIP

Handling your loan professionally now will make it easier to obtain and handle bank loans later. Getting familiar with promissory notes is great practice for the future, when you may want to ask banks and other institutional lenders for new funding. Sticking to a payment schedule—or understanding your cash flow well enough to anticipate problems and make arrangements for meeting your obligations—gets easier over time. And it's a practice that will come in handy when you're accountable to institutional lenders.

Start your drafting efforts with a quick read-through of the Sample Promissory Note for a $10,000 Amortized Loan to a Business, shown below. With an amortized loan, you pay the same amount each month (or other regular payment interval) with part of each payment going toward interest and the rest toward the principal (the amount owed). This is the same way you'll usually pay off a home mortgage (except your business loan will typically be much shorter repayment terms, such as three or four years). Although promissory notes vary in content and length, the sample below is in a widely accepted format and is relatively easy to follow. For more detailed, clause-by-clause explanations, see the sections that follow.

RELATED TOPICS
Chapter 6 includes key advice on how to make decisions about the interest rate, repayment schedule, collateral, and the like. Be sure to read it before drafting your promissory note.

If you're planning to arrange something other than an amortized loan, keep reading this section nonetheless. Most of the language used is common to any kind of promissory note, and I'll discuss adaptations you can make for other types of loans below.

RELATED TOPICS
Looking for the right sample promissory note? In addition to the sample promissory note provided below, you'll find a blank template for an amortized loan, as well as three others for graduated, interest-only, and seasonal loans in Appendix B and on the Loan Forms CD in the back of this book.

Sample Promissory Note for a
$10,000 Amortized Loan to a Business

Promissory Note (for an amortized loan)

1. **For Value Received,** Margaret Hollis ("Borrower") promises to pay to the order of Emily Hollis, of Chevy Chase, Maryland ("Lender"), the sum, in United States dollars, of ten thousand and 00/100 dollars ($10,000.00), plus interest accruing at an annual rate of twelve percent (12%) on the unpaid principal amount beginning on April 1, 2010 (the "Debt").

2. **Transferability.** Borrower understands that the Lender may transfer this Note. The Lender or anyone who takes this Note by Transfer and who is entitled to receive payments under this Note is called the "Note Holder" and will have the same rights and remedies as the Lender under this Note.

3. **Payments.** Payment of the Debt shall be made in monthly installments by personal check sent to 110 Tudor Road, Chevy Chase, Maryland. Payments shall include principal and interest, as follows:

   Beginning on October 1, 2010, and continuing monthly on the first of each month (the "Due Date") until September 1, 2013 (the "Final Due Date"), Borrower shall pay to the Lender or Note Holder the sum of $332.14 each month (the "Monthly Payment"). On the Final Due Date, Borrower shall pay all amounts remaining due under the terms of this Note.

   Attachment A lays out the payment schedule for this Note.

4. **Grace Period and Late Fee.** If the Borrower fails to make any payment in the full amount and within ten (10) calendar days (the "Grace Period") after the date it is due, Borrower agrees to pay a late charge to the Lender or Note Holder in the amount of $25.00 (the

Sample Promissory Note for a
$10,000 Amortized Loan to a Business (continued)

"Late Fee"). Borrower will pay this Late Fee promptly but only once on each late payment.

5. **Security.**

This is an unsecured note.

6. **Default and Acceleration.** If any installment payment due under this Note is not received by Lender within the Grace Period, the note will be in default and the entire amount of unpaid principal will become immediately due and payable at the option of Lender without prior notice of default to Borrower.

7. **Prepayment.** This Note may be prepaid in full at any time without cost or penalty to the Borrower.

8. **Attorneys' Fees.** If Lender prevails in a lawsuit to collect on this note, Borrower agrees to pay Lender's attorneys' fees in an amount the court finds to be just and reasonable.

9. **Waiver.** The undersigned and all other parties to this Note waive the following requirements:
   - presentment of the Note for payment by Lender
   - refusal of payment by Borrower after presentment of the Note by Lender, otherwise known as dishonor, and
   - Lender's notification to Borrower of Borrower's refusal to pay.

10. **Lender's Rights.** Lender's decision not to exercise a right or remedy under this Note at a given time does not waive the Lender's ability to exercise that right or remedy at a later date.

11. **Liability of Individual Borrowers.** The term "Borrower" may refer to one or more borrowers. If there is more than one borrower, they agree to be jointly and severally liable.

**Sample Promissory Note for a
$10,000 Amortized Loan to a Business (continued)**

12. **Governing Law.** This agreement will be governed by and construed in accordance with the laws of the state of Maryland.

Borrower's signature: *Margaret Hollis*

Print name: Margaret Hollis

Address: 5555 Craftsman, Baltimore, Maryland

Date: April 1, 2010

> **TIP**
> **What's with all the capital letters?** You might notice that the sample promissory note contains many capitalized words in parentheses and quotation marks, such as "Emily Hollis, of Chevy Chase, Maryland ("Lender")." This allows "Lender" to be used as shorthand for Emily throughout the note. Capitalizing the term is a legal custom, telling the reader that this term has been defined earlier and has the same meaning throughout the document.

Establishing the Debt, the Borrower, and the Lender

Clause 1. For Value Received

The sample promissory note starts off with some old-time legalese—"For Value Received." This phrase merely refers to the money or other assets the lender has already given (or, more likely, will be giving) you. It shows that you aren't just promising to send your lender monthly payments, but are doing so in return for money that the lender gave you first.

From the opening paragraph of the sample note, you learn that Margaret Hollis is borrowing $10,000 from Emily Hollis of Chevy Chase, Maryland. For simplicity's sake, the note refers to Margaret from now on as "Borrower." You also learn that Margaret promises to repay Emily (the "Lender") the principal amount plus 12% interest (the "Debt") that begins accruing on April 1, 2010.

You will need to tailor Clause 1 of the promissory note by filling in the following information:

- **Your name as ("Borrower") (and any coborrowers who will be signing the promissory note).** This will be your individual name if you are a sole proprietor. If you are a corporation, a partnership, or an LLC, see "Naming Your Business as the Borrower," below, for details.

> **TIP**
> **Name your business as the borrower whenever possible.** You'll waste any personal protection from liability that you've achieved if you are the borrower.

- **Lender's name and address.** Enter only city and state of residence.
- **Amount of the loan.** Spell out the amount and follow by bracketed numerals.
- **Interest rate.** Spell out the rate and follow by bracketed numerals.
- **Loan start date.** The date people insert here is usually either the loan start date (the date the note starts, as specified in the sample here) or the repayment start date (the date the first payment comes due).

Naming Your Business as the Borrower

If you want the loan to be to your business, name the business as the borrower in the opening paragraph of Clause 1, and sign on the business's behalf. Insert the following as the first line:

> **For Value Received**, [*name of your business*], a [*the U.S. state where your business was formed*] corporation/partnership/LLC with its principal place of business in [*city, state of business*] ("Borrower"), promises to pay ....

This language is separately included in Appendix B and on the Loan Forms CD—look for "Promissory Note Modifications for a Loan to a Business."

TIP

If the lender is not charging interest, be sure to read "Tax Liability if You Pay Too Little Interest" in Chapter 3. This explains that if the IRS learns of an interest-free loan, it can impute interest (that is assume that the lender has earned interest and will be required to report that interest as gift on that year's tax return). This won't be a problem if the total amount of gifts (including the interest which the IRS would impute) to the borrower in one calendar year is $13,000 or less.

Clause 2. Transferability

The second clause of the sample note contains what's called the "transfer provision." This allows the lender to sell the note and give the new holder the same rights as the original lender. While, technically, the new note holder could claim these rights anyway, this clause lets everyone know about this possibility in advance. You do not need to add anything to this clause.

Detailing Your Repayment Obligations

Clause 3. Payments (Amortized Loan)

The third clause of the promissory note provides more detail (probably the most detail of any clause) regarding your payment terms (typically, monthly, quarterly, or annually), when payment begins, the amount of each payment, and the repayment schedule. You'll need to have done all of your homework in Chapter 6 (determining the interest rate and so on) to fill in this clause.

The Sample Promissory Note for a $10,000 Amortized Loan to a Business tells us that over a three-year period—from October 1, 2010, to September 1, 2013 (after a six-month deferment of the loan repayment that began in April of 2010), the borrower needs to make monthly payments of $332.14, due on the first of each month. Margaret Hollis, the Borrower, agrees to send a personal check to Emily Hollis, to the Lender's home address, on this date (or you can put whatever options you agree to with the Lender, such as direct deposit). On the final due date, the note says, any outstanding amounts come due as well.

You will need to cover the following information in Clause 3:

- **The frequency of your payments.** Monthly, quarterly, annually, or in other periodic installments
- **Date the payment will begin and the day of the month each payment is due.** As in the sample promissory note, there may be a deferment period of several months after you sign the promissory note. And when creating your own promissory note, you don't necessarily have to choose the first of the month as your

repayment date. The 15th is another common choice. While some people prefer the 1st, in order to coincide with other bill paying (such as rent), others prefer the 15th specifically so as to gain a breather after paying all other bills.

- **The amount of money you will pay each installment period.** You'll figure this out with a loan calculator as explained in "Creating Your Repayment Schedule," below.
- **The repayment schedule.** I recommend you attach the full repayment schedule (see the samples later in the chapter) and label it accordingly (such as Attachment A).
- **Details as to where/how you will make each payment.** This might be a check mailed to the lender's home address or direct deposit into the lender's bank account.

How to Prepare Attachments to Your Promissory Note

Your promissory note should contain all of the terms of your agreement with the lender. But rather than putting everything in the promissory note itself, you will want to prepare attachments, specifically for the repayment period and the security agreement (if any). Just make sure your promissory note clearly refers to each attachment and that each attachment clearly refers back to the promissory note. For example, you might label the repayment schedule (referred to in Clause 3) as Attachment A, then refer to the security agreement, if any (referred to in Clause 5) as Attachment B, and so on. Staple all attachments to the promissory note.

Clause 3. Payments (Not Amortized Types of Loans)

If you and your lender agree to a repayment schedule other than an amortized one, such as a graduated, seasonal, or interest-only schedule, replace the amortized language in Clause 3 of the sample above with the appropriate language from the options below (also available in Appendix B and on the Loan Forms CD at the back of this book). You'll need to have a copy of your repayment schedule handy, preferably one generated by a loan calculator, so that you can easily insert the specific amounts and due dates that make up your repayment. (See "Creating Your Repayment Schedule" at the end of this chapter, for advice.) Follow the advice under "Clause 3. Payments (Amortized Loan)," above, regarding other information you need to cover in Clause 3 (such as where payments are due and the repayment schedule).

Graduated. The following language describes a graduated repayment schedule for the same loan as described in the sample note ($10,000 at 12% interest for a three-year term). Notice that because it is a graduated loan, there are two steps (or increases) in the payment amount—with three "platforms" or "payment levels"—and that each step lasts for one year of 12 monthly payments, with the first and last date of that amount specified.

Beginning on October 1, 2010, and continuing monthly on the first of each month through September 1, 2011, Borrower shall pay to Lender on the first of every month the sum of $238.89.

Then, beginning on October 1, 2011, and continuing monthly on the first of each month through September 1, 2012, Borrower shall pay to Lender on the first of every month the sum of $361.11.

Finally, beginning on October 1, 2012, and continuing monthly on the first of each month until September 1, 2013, Borrower shall pay to Lender on the first of every month the sum of $466.67.

On September 1, 2013, (Final Due Date), Borrower shall pay all amounts remaining due under the terms of this Note.

Seasonal. For a seasonal repayment schedule, the amount you pay varies depending on the season. If, for example, you own a café that is located on a college campus, it might be busy nine months out of the year, but very slow during the summer months when students have vacated the campus. A customized seasonal repayment schedule for your cafe could have nine months of high-season payments that correspond to the school schedule and then switch to a low-season schedule of reduced payments for the summer months, when revenue is low or even zero if the business temporarily closes. Use language like the following:

> Borrower shall make monthly payments as described below:
>
> For the calendar months of September, October, November, December, January, February, March, April, and May of each year, Borrower shall pay on the first day of each month the sum of $429.52 to the Lender or Note Holder ("High-Season Monthly Payment").
>
> For the calendar months of June, July, and August of each calendar year, Borrower shall pay on the first day of each month the sum of $159.95 to the Lender or Note Holder ("Low-Season Monthly Payment").
>
> Finally, on September 1, 2013 ("Final Due Date"), Borrower shall pay all amounts remaining due under the terms of this Note.

Interest-only. If you are drafting a promissory note for an interest-only loan (one in which you will make payments of all interest and no principal for the life of the loan, then pay the entire principal back on the final due date), use language like the following:

> Borrower will pay all interest that accrues during the term of the loan by making a payment every month. Borrower will make monthly payments on the first day of each month beginning on October 1, 2010. Borrower will make these payments every month until Borrower has paid all of the interest and any other charges described below that Borrower may owe under this Note. Each monthly payment will be applied as of its scheduled due date and will be applied to interest before principal. On September 1, 2013 ("Maturity Date"), Borrower will pay all remaining principal, interest, and any other amounts due to Lender under the terms of this Note.

As you can see, you can write the language in the promissory note to fit just about any repayment schedule you can come up with—for example, if you make one lump sum payment with (or without) interest after a period of months or years when your business is better established.

Penalties for Late Payments

Clause 4. Grace Period and Late Fee

The promissory note spells out the grace period (the number of days you have after the due date to make your payment without being considered late), and the late fee ($25 in the sample). When payment is made beyond your grace period, you must include the stated late fee.

Most people negotiate a grace period of between seven and 15 days and a late fee charge of $25 if the payment is made after the grace period expires. Since this is a private loan, you and your lender can choose any grace period or fee you mutually think appropriate, or none at all (just be very clear as to all the details, such as whether the late fee escalates after a certain number of days). The sample note is gentle on the borrower, by allowing a ten-day grace period after the payment was initially due (but note that it's ten calendar days, not business days—weekends and holidays count).

> EXAMPLE: Nicole knows she has a tendency to pay bills a few days late. After her brother said he'd lend her $4,000 to start her graphic design business, she asked that the promissory note contain a 15-day grace period. Her brother, however, didn't want to spend a whole 15 days wondering whether she was ever going to pay and suggested a seven-day grace period. To reach a compromise, they agreed to a ten-day grace period but with a $75 late fee. That way, Nicole has the flexibility she wants, while the late payment penalty increases her brother's chances of getting paid in a timely fashion.

CAUTION

One day after the payment due date, you're late. Inexperienced entrepreneurs have been known to drop the check in the mail on the due date, which means that by the time the check arrives, late fees may already be due (unless there's a grace period). Don't make this mistake; mail your payments several days before they're due or set up direct debit.

How the Note Addresses a Secured Loan

Clause 5. Security

If your loan is unsecured (such as the sample shown here), you simply need to check off the unsecured loan box in Clause 5.

But if you're planning on securing your loan, this is the portion of the promissory note where you'll describe the asset and put your collateral on the line.

If you secure your note with collateral—in other words, if you promise to give up a business or personal asset to fulfill the debt obligation if you can't repay it in cash—you must, of course, check the other box in Clause 5, for secured loans. Below that, there's space for you to add key identifying information describing the collateral you've offered, such as the type of property, the manufacturer, the model, the year, an ID number, and the color. Note that you don't need to include a dollar value. Cars, computers, and equipment are the most common items people list as collateral.

> EXAMPLE: Your collateral descriptions might look like one of these:
> - 2007 Dodge Durango, license number A2345678, Vehicle Identification Number JKLM1234567890, or
> - Three Acme natural gas-powered heat lamps, serial numbers: 1234567890; 2234567890; and 3234567890.

In addition to filling out this portion of Clause 5 of the note, you'll separately need to do two things:

1. **Prepare a separate security agreement.** This agreement can be prepared without an attorney. Its purpose is simply to identify the collateral you wish to use and agree that it will become the property of the lender if you are unable to repay the loan. A blank form security agreement is provided in Appendix B and

on the Loan Forms CD. See "How to Complete the Security Agreement" and the sample security agreement, below.

2. **File a UCC Financing Statement with the appropriate state agency.** (The lender will sometimes want to do this to record his or her security interest in your property.) The Uniform Commercial Code (UCC) Financing Statement is a one-page form that you can obtain from the office of the secretary of state in the state where your business is located. (To find yours, see the website of the National Association of Secretaries of State (NASS) at www. nass.org.) The UCC form happens to be identical from state to state, so you can also use the one in Appendix B and on the CD-ROM. The form is simple, requiring merely the borrower's and lender's names and contact information, and a description of the collateral. After you've completed the UCC Financing Statement, all 50 states now require that you file it in the office of your secretary of state. This filing makes the statement available to any member of the public who wants to find out what liens are being held against your business's assets.

But which state is "yours," if your business operates in more than one? File your UCC form in the state in which (1) you are a resident, if your business is not incorporated, or (2) your business was incorporated (or formed, if it's another entity such as an LLC).

For example, if your business was incorporated in Delaware, but your office is in Massachusetts, you should file the UCC Financing Statement with the secretary of state in Delaware. In some states, you must also attach a copy of the security agreement. To find your state's requirements, contact the secretary of state's office directly, or check whether it has posted this information online at a state government website.

You probably won't be surprised to hear that most states charge a filing fee, ranging from $50 to $100.

How to Complete the Security Agreement

Fill in the clauses as follows:

- **Grant of Security Interest.** In Clause 1, insert information from the promissory note (description of the property that will be used as collateral, and the date, amount and annual percentage rate).
- **Financial Statement.** Clause 2 states that the note will be secured by a UCC Financing Statement and that you (the borrower) will sign any additional documents needed to protect the lender's security interest (this may be necessary for certain kinds of assets, such as cars).
- **Use and Care of Secured Property, Borrower's Default, Lender's Rights, etc.** The remaining clauses (numbers 3–13) of the security agreement cover your care and use of the property secured (for example, you agree not to sell the property and to pay all taxes as they become due), state when you will be considered in default (you'll need to agree on the number of days), and describe what the lender can do if you default.

After completing the security agreement, both you and the lender should sign and date the last page, following the signing instructions below for the promissory note. (But in the case of the security agreement, both you and the lender sign, unlike the promissory note which only you, the borrower, sign.) Attach the security agreement to the original promissory note which goes to the lender. Keep copies for yourself.

Security Agreement

Name of Borrower: _____

Name of Lender: _____

1. **Grant of Security Interest.** Borrower grants to Lender a continuing security interest in the following personal property: _____

   _____

   _____

   (the Secured Property). Borrower grants this security interest to secure performance of the promissory note dated _____ that Borrower executed in favor of Lender (the Note), which obligates Borrower to pay Lender $ _____ with interest at the rate of _____% per year, on the terms stated in the Note.

2. **Financing Statement.** Until the amount due under the Note is paid in full, the Note will be further secured by a Uniform Commercial Code (UCC) Financing Statement. Borrower agrees to sign any other documents that Lender reasonably requests to protect Lender's security interest in the Secured Property.

3. **Use and Care of Secured Property.** Until the amount due under the Note is paid in full, Borrower agrees to:
   A. maintain the Secured Property in good repair
   B. not sell, transfer, or release the Secured Property without Lender's prior written consent
   C. pay all taxes on the Secured Property as they become due, and
   D. allow Lender to inspect the Secured Property at any reasonable time.

4. **Borrower's Default.** If Borrower is more than _____ days late in making any payment due under the Note, or if Buyer fails to correct any violations of Paragraph 3, within _____ days of receiving written notice from Lender, Borrower will be in default.

5. **Lender's Rights.** If Borrower is in default, Lender may exercise the remedies contained in the UCC for the state of _____ and any other remedies legally available to Lender. Before exercising such remedies, Lender will provide at least ten days' advance notice, as provided in Paragraph 6. Lender may, for example:

   A. remove the Secured Property from the place where it is then located

   B. require Borrower to make the Secured Property available to Lender at a place designated by Lender that is reasonably convenient to Borrower and Lender, or

   C. sell, lease, or otherwise dispose of the Secured Property.

6. **Notice.** Any notice may be delivered to a party at the address that follows a party's signature below, or to a new address that a party designates in writing. A notice may be delivered:

   A. in person

   B. by certified mail, or

   C. by overnight courier.

7. **Entire Agreement.** This is the entire agreement between the parties. It replaces and supersedes any and all oral agreements between the parties, as well as any prior writings.

8. **Successors and Assigns.** This agreement binds and benefits the parties' heirs, successors, and assigns.

9. **Governing Law.** This agreement will be governed by and construed in accordance with the laws of the state of _____ .

10. **Counterparts.** The parties may sign several identical counterparts of this agreement. Any fully signed counterpart shall be treated as an original.

11. **Modification.** This agreement may be modified only in writing.

12. **Waiver.** If one party waives any term or provision of this agreement at any time, that waiver will be effective only for the specific instance and specific purpose for which the waiver was given. If either party fails to exercise or delays exercising any of its rights

or remedies under this agreement, that party retains the right to enforce that term or provision at a later time.

13. **Severability.** If any court determines that any provision of this agreement is invalid or unenforceable, any such invalidity or unenforceability will affect only that provision and will not make any other provision of this agreement invalid or unenforceable and such provision shall be modified, amended, or limited only to the extent necessary to render it valid and enforceable.

_____   _____
Lender's Signature   Date

_____
Print name

_____
Address

_____
Address

_____   _____
Borrower's Signature   Date

_____
Print name

_____
Address

_____
Address

CAUTION

Do not use the security agreement included in Appendix B and on the CD-ROM if the collateral is real estate or intellectual property (copyright, patent, or trademark). This form is intended only for tangible personal property. If you pledge your home or other real estate as security for a loan, a security agreement won't be adequate to protect the lender. A well-informed lender will ask you to sign a mortgage or a deed of trust, which can then be recorded (filed) with a designated county official to establish the lender's security interest in the real estate. Because title to real estate is a highly technical matter, you should seek the assistance of a real estate lawyer before signing a mortgage or deed of trust. For similar reasons, you should consult an intellectual property lawyer for help in pledging intangible personal property, such as a copyright, trademark, or patent, as security for a loan.

How the Note Penalizes Your Nonpayment

Clause 6. Default and Acceleration

Clause 6 of the promissory note travels into "may-not-happen" territory and is intended to protect the lender in case you have trouble keeping up your end of the bargain. Even if you have every intention of making your payments, agreeing on what will happen if you can't make a payment (even within the grace period) is one of the best ways to forestall later disputes. The note describes nonpayment as a "default," which is a legal term meaning your failure to perform a legal duty. (In a more-complicated transaction, the promissory note might describe several types of default, but in this note, nonpayment is the only one.)

The penalty if you default on this note is that the entire unpaid amount comes due. This is often known as an "acceleration" clause. Although it sounds harsh, it's a traditional clause, and only fair to the lender—without it, he or she would end up having to separately sue you for each payment as it came due, regardless of the fact that you're clearly in default and probably not able to make these future payments.

EXAMPLE: Arnold borrowed $15,000 from his brother to start a vitamin drink business, to be paid back over three years. He made the first two payments, but then a slick new competitor grabbed away his growing customer base, and Arnold missed the next three payments. With 31 payments to go, Arnold's business went bankrupt. The acceleration clause makes the remainder of the debt all come due so that Arnold's brother can, if he wishes, act to collect the full amount owed instead of having to wait out the term of the loan.

Fortunately, very few family and friend lenders would begin collections as early as a few days after you've missed your first payment. Most family and friend lenders think of default as the point at which the borrower finally tells the lender that he or she can't make any more payments, no matter what the note says.

Clause 6 also mentions that the lender can choose whether or not to exercise the acceleration clause—but can exercise it without giving the borrower a last chance to pay up.

TIP
Nothing in the sample note forces the lender to sue you over a default. The note gives the lender discretion. That means that you can talk to your lender about the probability that you won't be able to make your upcoming payments and agree to a plan regarding those missed payments—which, legally, will then mean you are not in default.

Protecting Your Right to Prepay

Clause 7. Prepayment

Though it contains only one short sentence, Clause 7 is one that you should insist upon including. This is generally known as a "prepayment clause" and gives you the right to pay ahead or pay off the entire loan at once, with no "cost or penalty." The time may come when you've received a cash influx and can benefit financially from paying off this loan and perhaps later looking for more-advantageous financing elsewhere.

> EXAMPLE: Jerry had three years left on a loan he received from his uncle. However, Jerry's music store had been doing extremely well, thanks to a series of in-store events. By exercising his prepayment clause rights, he paid his uncle the unpaid balance of the loan and saved himself a number of future interest payments. Two years later, he was able to borrow a much larger amount from a bank, at a reasonable interest rate, for a deposit on a second store.

Deciding Who Pays the Attorneys

Clause 8. Attorneys' Fees

Clause 8 of the promissory note could be called the "kick-you-when-you're-down" clause, though it's more officially known as the "attorneys' fees clause." It states that you will be responsible for any legal fees that the lender racks up in order to collect what you owe (assuming you end up in a legal dispute and the lender wins). This tool is a traditional form of protection for you to provide the lender. But keep in mind that under the laws of some states, this type of clause will be read by a court to go both ways: This means that if you (the borrower) win a legal dispute with the lender, you will be entitled to attorney fees and court costs, even if your promissory note or loan papers don't specifically say so.

Easing the Collections Process for the Lender

Clause 9. Waiver

Clause 9, known as the waiver clause, is a standard legal clause in the lending industry. It unfortunately does away with some of the borrower protections that banks traditionally had to comply with to collect on a bad loan. These protections were basically legal formalities, including a series of back-and-forth notices regarding the amount owed and the borrower's refusals to pay (called presentments and dishonors). The purpose of the clause is to speed up the process of collecting on the loan once it's clear that the borrower is unable or unwilling to make the scheduled payments.

If your lender is confused by the old-fashioned language in this clause, you can, in good conscience, reassure him or her that the clause is more to the lender's advantage than to yours! Nevertheless, there's no sense in trying to avoid this clause, because it is standard, and using it shows that you won't be trying to impede the lender's efforts to collect.

Clause 10. Lender's Rights

Clause 10, which I headed "Lender's Rights," is also sometimes known as a "non-waiver clause" and offers an additional form of protection for your lender. This clause says that just because your lender may give you a break on one payment, perhaps by accepting a late payment without charging a late fee, that doesn't change the lender's overall rights, in this case to receive your payments on time and charge a late fee. In other words, the fact that in one instance your lender doesn't insist that you completely adhere to the terms of the note doesn't let you claim, "Since it was okay that one time, it must be okay all the time!"

Sharing Your Liability With Coborrowers

Clause 11. Liability of Individual Borrowers

Clause 11 says that if you sign the note with fellow borrowers, such as a partner in your business, you are each liable individually for the full amount of the debt. If one borrower can't pay, the other owes the entire amount, not just a portion of it.

Which State's Law Governs

Clause 12. Governing Law

Clause 12 is standard in promissory notes and many other contracts. It simply says that if any points of contention arise out of the agreement, the laws of the state named in the clause will be used to resolve the conflict.

Insert the name of the state—this is usually where the asset is located which is usually where the borrower lives.

Signing the Promissory Note: Individual and Sole Proprietor Borrowers

The last portion of the sample note is called the "signature block." You (the Borrower) must sign the promissory note for it to be valid. (You'll do this after you finalize all details as described under "How to Close the Deal for a Private Loan," below.) Whoever signs here becomes liable for the debt. If you are borrowing the money as an individual (as in the sample note), or if your business is a sole proprietorship, then you will sign the note and accept personal responsibility.

If your business is incorporated, an LLC, or a partnership, the business is the borrower and you must make sure to sign on behalf of the business. (See "Signing the Promissory Note: Business Borrower," below.) As long as you sign correctly, the business is liable for the debt, but you are not.

Print out one copy of the promissory note. You and any other borrower should sign and date only one copy of the document and provide your address in the space provided. The signed original should be given to the lender, and you should keep a copy of the signed promissory note for your own records.

> **TIP**
>
> **Only the borrower needs to sign the promissory note.** Since the promissory note represents your promise to pay, it requires only your signature to be legally binding. Sometimes lenders feel like they should be signing something, too. Actually, they shouldn't. By signing, the lender might call into question whether the document really is a note (representing an obligation owed) instead of some other type of legal document, such as a contract (which has a whole separate set of purposes and uses).

Signing the Promissory Note: Business Borrower

If your business will be the borrower on the promissory note, you'll need to use a different signature block from the one on the sample note. Instead, you'll need to list:

- the name of the company that is the borrower, and
- the state where the business is legally established and the type of legal entity (such as corporation, partnership, or LLC).

Sign and print your name (and your official title) and fill in the address of your company and the date when you are signing the promissory note. See the "Sample Signature Block for a Business," below.

Sample Signature Block for a Business

Borrower: _Hood Marketing and Design, a Texas Limited Liability_
Company

By: _Lee Hood_

Print name: _Lee Hood_

Title: _Member_

Address: _125 Elm Street, Dallas, Texas_

Date: _March 3, 2010_

TIP

If loaning money to an incorporated business makes your lender anxious, you can offer to be a coborrower with your business. That way, if you fail to make payments, both the corporation and you can be held liable. This is a shorthand way of avoiding having you make a personal guarantee, an alternative requiring fairly complicated documentation. You can be a coborrower simply by adding yourself as a signing party to the promissory note and adding your name, rather than just your company's name, as the borrowing party.

Notarization of Promissory Note

Some lenders may want a notary public to witness your signing of the promissory note. If it makes your lender happy, do it, but it's not necessary to make the document legally binding. (All a notary public really does is confirm the identity of the person signing the document, and your lender should know who you are by now.) Add the following language (available in Appendix B and on the Loan Forms CD) to your note for the notary's use.

Certificate of Acknowledgment of Notary Public

State of _____

County of _____

On _____, before me, _____

_____, a notary public in and for said state,

personally appeared _____, who proved to me on the basis of satisfactory evidence to be the person whose name is subscribed to the within instrument and acknowledged to me that he or she executed the same in his or her authorized capacity and that by his or her signature on the instrument, the person, or the entity upon behalf of which the person acted, executed the instrument.

WITNESS my hand and official seal.

_____

Notary Public for the State of _____

My commission expires _____

[NOTARY SEAL]

How to Close the Deal for a Private Loan

At last, it's time for you to collect the funding you've worked so hard to line up. If you have ever bought a home, you've probably experienced a "closing." It's traditionally a meeting where both parties (and, in many states, their attorneys) sit together around a conference table to sign legal documents and exchange checks. Although bringing everyone together in this way is the ideal, it's not always realized with business loans.

Especially if you have friends and family located in different parts of the country, doing the closing in person may be impossible. With fax machines, FedEx, and wire transfers, not to mention cell phones, the business of signing documents and transferring funds can now be adequately accomplished from a distance. Don't worry if the signing of documents and the transfer of funds don't happen simultaneously; the important thing is that they both happen.

> **TIP**
>
> **If your scheduling allows it, try to close the deal in person.** It lends a professional air to the transaction. But don't force it: Do what's easiest and most comfortable for you and your lender.

To close the deal, take the following steps:

1. **Draft a promissory note (along with a repayment schedule) based on terms agreed to by the lender and send the draft note and schedule to the lender.** Email is fine for drafts and preferable if it speeds up the process. Have your lender review the draft promissory note and repayment schedule and comment on any financial terms that do not appear as he or she expected or mention any other problems (like misspellings).

2. **Make agreed-upon changes and prepare the final copy of the promissory note and repayment schedule—or share a second draft with your lender if the comments on the first draft were substantial.**

3. **Sign the final promissory note (remember that typically only the borrower needs to sign) and attach the repayment schedule and signed security agreement (if any).** Keep a copy for your records, and send the original back to the lender for safekeeping. Don't sign any additional copies—that will only confuse matters. Later, when the note has been repaid, you are entitled to get back the original, because the obligation no longer exists.

4. **Congratulations! Accept payment from your lender!** Your lender will disburse the funds—typically by a personal check, cashier's check, or wire transfer. If you accept a personal check, note that the clearing period may be longer than usual due to the large amount.

CAUTION

Don't be surprised by last-minute changes of mind. I've known lenders to call shortly before a closing date and call the whole thing off because the lender has changed his or her mind, the lender's spouse has vetoed the deal, or the lender's tax bill was higher than expected. The only one I haven't heard yet is that the lender's dog ate the paperwork. Some lenders just get cold feet. If you really feel that the lender is someone you want associated with your business, don't give up. Of course, if the lender is a close friend or family member, or you sense you might hurt your relationship, don't exert too much pressure.

Creating Your Repayment Schedule

Chapter 6 (the section called "When and How Do You Want to Repay?") explains your different options for repayment schedules, and how you'll probably go back and forth a few times before reaching final agreement with your lender. Referring to the final version of your promissory note, use a loan calculator (also explained in Chapter 6) to generate a final repayment schedule. The schedule will tell you the due date for each payment and the total payment due. It will also break each payment down into its two components: principal and interest.

> CAUTION
>
> **It's easy to mistakenly rely on a draft repayment schedule.** While you were still discussing options with your lender, you probably had a few draft repayment schedules floating around. And even if you thought you had a final schedule, but you and your lender made a last-minute adjustment to the loan start date, perhaps advancing it by a week, that would have thrown off the whole repayment schedule. Double check that you're using the latest version.

Print out the final schedule and keep it handy—tape it to your wall, write reminders on your calendar, and do whatever else you have to do to stay on top of your obligation. (Of course, if you do direct debit, you won't have to remember to mail a check each month.) While an amortized schedule might be easy to remember (in which, for example, you owe $200 each month on the 1st of the month), other types of schedules might not be so obvious or unchanging. Whatever your schedule, a loan log (discussed in Chapter 10) will help you keep on track.

To get used to reading your repayment schedule, look at the samples below. (I also showed a few samples back in Chapter 6.) The first sample shows an amortized $10,000 loan with 8% interest due over a period of two years. As you'll see from the table, each monthly payment of $452.27 goes toward paying down both the principal and the interest on the loan.

Sample Repayment Schedule for Amortized Loan				
Payment Number	Due Date	Principal	Interest	Total
1	2/1/2010	$385.60	$66.67	$452.27
2	3/1/2010	388.17	64.10	452.27
3	4/1/2010	390.76	61.51	452.27
4	5/1/2010	393.37	58.90	452.27
5	6/1/2010	395.99	56.28	452.27
6	7/1/2010	398.63	53.64	452.27
7	8/1/2010	401.29	50.98	452.27
8	9/1/2010	403.96	48.31	452.27
9	10/1/2010	406.66	45.61	452.27
10	11/1/2010	409.37	42.90	452.27
11	12/1/2010	412.10	40.17	452.27
12	1/1/2011	414.84	37.43	452.27
13	2/1/2011	417.61	34.66	452.27
14	3/1/2011	420.39	31.88	452.27
15	4/1/2011	423.19	29.08	452.27
16	5/1/2011	426.02	26.25	452.27
17	6/1/2011	428.86	23.41	452.27
18	7/1/2011	431.72	20.55	452.27
19	8/1/2011	434.59	17.68	452.27
20	9/1/2011	437.49	14.78	452.27
21	10/1/2011	440.41	11.86	452.27
22	11/1/2011	443.34	8.93	452.27
23	12/1/2011	446.30	5.97	452.27
24	1/1/2012	449.34	3.00	452.34
	Total	$10,000.00	$854.55	$10,854.55

The next sample repayment schedule is for a seasonal loan. It shows you how repayment amounts would vary on a two-year, $10,000 loan with 8% interest where monthly payments were set higher during the expected busy season, and lower during the slow season. If you've signed onto such a loan, you'll need to keep track of what month you're in and what amount is due.

Sample Repayment Schedule for Seasonal Loan				
Payment Number	Due Date	Principal	Interest	Total
1	2/1/2010	$250.00	$50.00	$300.00
2	3/1/2010	250.00	50.00	300.00
3	4/1/2010	250.00	50.00	300.00
4	5/1/2010	250.00	50.00	300.00
5	6/1/2010	750.00	50.00	800.00
6	7/1/2010	750.00	50.00	800.00
7	8/1/2010	750.00	50.00	800.00
8	9/1/2010	750.00	50.00	800.00
9	10/1/2010	250.00	50.00	300.00
10	11/1/2010	250.00	50.00	300.00
11	12/1/2010	250.00	50.00	300.00
12	1/1/2011	250.00	50.00	300.00
13	2/1/2011	250.00	50.00	300.00
14	3/1/2011	250.00	50.00	300.00
15	4/1/2011	250.00	50.00	300.00
16	5/1/2011	250.00	50.00	300.00
17	6/1/2011	750.00	50.00	800.00
18	7/1/2011	750.00	50.00	800.00
19	8/1/2011	750.00	50.00	800.00
20	9/1/2011	750.00	50.00	800.00
21	10/1/2011	250.00	50.00	300.00
22	11/1/2011	250.00	50.00	300.00
23	12/1/2011	250.00	50.00	300.00
24	1/1/2012	250.00	50.00	300.00
	Total	$10,000.00	$1,200.00	$11,200.00

The next sample repayment table is for a graduated loan, which starts low and increases step by step over time. The following schedule shows a $10,000, two-year loan with a graduated repayment plan with two steps. The payments will change after the first year. Just when the borrower is getting used to one amount, it will to shift to a higher one. Again, you'll want to keep such a table someplace handy, such as your electronic calendar, so you don't lose track of those changing amounts.

Sample Repayment Schedule for a Graduated Loan				
Payment Number	Due Date	Principal	Interest	Total
1	2/1/2010	$277.78	$66.67	$344.44
2	3/1/2010	277.78	66.67	344.44
3	4/1/2010	277.78	66.67	344.44
4	5/1/2010	277.78	66.67	344.44
5	6/1/2010	277.78	66.67	344.44
6	7/1/2010	277.78	66.67	344.44
7	8/1/2010	277.78	66.67	344.44
8	9/1/2010	277.78	66.67	344.44
9	10/1/2010	277.78	66.67	344.44
10	11/1/2010	277.78	66.67	344.44
11	12/1/2010	277.78	66.67	344.44
12	1/1/2011	277.78	66.67	344.44
13	2/1/2011	555.56	44.44	600.00
14	3/1/2011	555.56	44.44	600.00
15	4/1/2011	555.56	44.44	600.00
16	5/1/2011	555.56	44.44	600.00
17	6/1/2011	555.56	44.44	600.00
18	7/1/2011	555.56	44.44	600.00
19	8/1/2011	555.56	44.44	600.00
20	9/1/2011	555.56	44.44	600.00
21	10/1/2011	555.56	44.44	600.00
22	11/1/2011	555.56	44.44	600.00
23	12/1/2011	555.56	44.44	600.00
24	1/1/2012	555.56	44.44	600.00
	Total	$10,000.00	$1,333.33	$11,333.33

The last sample repayment schedule shows an interest-only loan, again for $10,000 over two years. You'll see that while monthly payments remain low, the last payment will include a much larger balloon payment—which you wouldn't want to forget is coming.

Sample Repayment Schedule for an Interest-Only Loan				
Payment Number	**Due Date**	**Principal**	**Interest**	**Total**
1	2/1/2010	$0.00	$66.67	$66.67
2	3/1/2010	0.00	66.67	66.67
3	4/1/2010	0.00	66.67	66.67
4	5/1/2010	0.00	66.67	66.67
5	6/1/2010	0.00	66.67	66.67
6	7/1/2010	0.00	66.67	66.67
7	8/1/2010	0.00	66.67	66.67
8	9/1/2010	0.00	66.67	66.67
9	10/1/2010	0.00	66.67	66.67
10	11/1/2010	0.00	66.67	66.67
11	12/1/2010	0.00	66.67	66.67
12	1/1/2011	0.00	66.67	66.67
13	2/1/2011	0.00	66.67	66.67
14	3/1/2011	0.00	66.67	66.67
15	4/1/2011	0.00	66.67	66.67
16	5/1/2011	0.00	66.67	66.67
17	6/1/2011	0.00	66.67	66.67
18	7/1/2011	0.00	66.67	66.67
19	8/1/2011	0.00	66.67	66.67
20	9/1/2011	0.00	66.67	66.67
21	10/1/2011	0.00	66.67	66.67
22	11/1/2011	0.00	66.67	66.67
23	12/1/2011	0.00	66.67	66.67
24	1/1/2012	10,000.00	66.67	10,066.67
	Total	**$10,000.00**	**$1,600.00**	**$11,600.00**

How to Change a Promissory Note

If, after you've signed the promissory note, you and the borrower agree to change a term, you must put your new agreement in writing. If it's a matter of simply changing one clause of the promissory note, you can prepare an amendment like this:

Agreement to Modify Promissory Note

Margaret Hollis (Borrower) and Emily Hollis (Lender) agree to modify the promissory note (Note) dated April 1, 2010, under which Borrower agrees to pay to Lender the sum of $10,000, plus interest accruing at an annual rate of 12% on the unpaid principal amount beginning on October 1, 2010. Lender and Borrower agree to change the late fee (Clause 4. Grace Period and Late Fee) from $25 to $45. All other terms of the Note will remain in effect.

Both you and the lender should sign and date the agreement to modify the promissory note. The lender should keep the original signed document and give you a copy.

For more substantial changes, such as major changes in the repayment schedule, you should prepare a new promissory note that cancels the old one. See "Changing Your Repayment Schedule and Preparing a New Promissory Note" in Chapter 10 for details.

How to Be Your Own Investor Relations Department

FORMS ON CD-ROM

Chapter 10 includes instructions for, and a sample of, the following form, which is in Appendix B and on the Loan Forms CD included at the back of this book:

- Loan Log

N ow that you've lined up your financing, your main task is to throw yourself into managing and growing your business, right? Well, yes and no. Unless you also keep a watchful eye on your obligations to the people who helped fund your business in the first place, they may think you just took the money and ran. Good relations require open, honest, and regular communications with your lenders—more than just putting a check in the mail once a month.

This chapter shows you how to update your lenders and gift-givers on your business progress, and (in the case of loans), how to repay responsibly and in an organized way (with a loan log and year-end reports). Since starting and running a business is not always smooth sailing, this chapter also covers how to deal with difficult problems that may come up along the way, such as missing a payment (or, in the worst case, having to default on the loan).

Communicating Your Progress to Lenders

There's a funny human tendency to think that, when you sign a legal agreement, you need not—or perhaps even should not—do anything outside of that agreement. The promissory note you signed for your lender mostly talks about dates, payments, and fees. Without a doubt, the obligation to repay is a crucial one. But imagine what your lender will think if you call only with plaintive cries for help or requests to make late payments. If you really want to keep the relationship strong, keep in touch during good times, as well. For example, let your lender know when you've reached key milestones or signed up big customers. Many entrepreneurs use email newsletters, blogs, or social networking tools to keep their supporters updated.

People who made gifts or loans won't expect you to provide detailed business information, but would appreciate a friendly message once in a while. Here are some ways to make casual, but ideally regular, contact with these folks.

In-Person Updates

For relatives and friends you see regularly, such as at family dinners or social events, you'll quite naturally want to tell them how your business is doing. For other people with whom you have a personal relationship, you might want to invite them to lunch or coffee. Don't turn your update into a lecture—but think ahead about any fun facts or interesting stories you might share with this person. This is all some lenders will need.

Holiday Cards

Businesses of all sizes use holiday cards as a way to cast a wide net of appreciation, once a year, to key customers, suppliers, business partners, and, yes, lenders. If you haven't done so already, start a holiday mailing list and put every last one of your lenders' and investors' names on it. You can pick up a few boxes of cards at the store and fill them out by hand for friends and family. For other investors, you might want to go to websites that offer printed cards with a custom greeting and the name of your business (or make your own, if you're the creative type).

Customer Mailings

If you hold a grand opening of your business, make sure your lenders get an invitation. As time goes on, some entrepreneurs also include their lenders in mailings they make to customers, announcing new products, sales and other special events, and more. If, for example, you own an art gallery, your lenders would probably be interested in announcements of your art openings. If you own a café that features live music, they might appreciate receiving a schedule.

Press Clippings

Whenever you receive coverage in the press—whether it's the local paper or *The New York Times*—make good-quality copies of the clipping and share it. Attach a simple, handwritten note saying that you thought the person might be interested in seeing that your business is getting some public recognition. Many press articles are now available online—if yours are, you might choose to send an email link rather than a printed version, to save time and money.

A favorable review of your new restaurant or bakery is, for example, a great piece of news to share. As you accumulate clippings, you'll soon share only the best ones, but you should keep track of the rest, anyway.

Most businesses dedicate a page on their website to press coverage. Also, favorable quotations from these sources look great added to your business plan, executive summary, or loan request letter.

Online Updates

Rather than sending email newsletters, entrepreneurs often use more interactive ways to share information with supporters. Blogs are perhaps the most popular because they provide the same level of control over content that an email newsletter would provide, but also invite readers into the conversation. Social networking sites, such as Facebook, allow you to share your business updates with your friends and family at the same time as your lenders.

TIP

Good news is best, but some bad news should be shared, too. Don't feel like your supporters only want to hear from you when business is booming and you've just landed a big new customer account. If, for example, a competitor has opened shop down the street, your lenders might be interested in knowing about this wrench in your plan and have advice on dealing with it.

Repaying Responsibly

Your ongoing job as a borrower—at least, when it comes to basic legal or other requirements—is relatively straightforward. To avoid embarrassment (and potential disasters), know when and where your payments are due and make them on time.

Of course, you have every intention of fulfilling your financial obligations to your lender by making your payments as promised. Follow the repayment schedule we recommend you prepare and attach to your promissory note (see Chapter 9), and be clear about the logistics of making your payments, such as mailing a check to your lender's home address or making a direct deposit to your lender's bank account. You and your lender should have already agreed to these in your promissory note. If these important terms weren't spelled out in your promissory note, you and your lender must agree to a procedure and arrange the details *before* the first payment comes due. The best time to do this is at the closing, when the promissory note and the money change hands.

Take the time to read your copy of the promissory note again. Hopefully, by using this book, you've already drafted a note that is written in plain English and understandable to the average reader. Make sure there are no surprises and that you know how and when to fulfill the obligation it represents.

Motown Records Began With a Loan From a Family Member

In 1959, the founder of Motown Records, Berry Gordy, Jr., was working on the Ford assembly line in Detroit and writing and producing songs on the side. He had an extraordinary eye for talent and decided to start his own record company, for which he borrowed $800 from his family. He called it "Tamla Records." Some minor and major hits followed. Gordy separately launched Motown records a few years later, and the company became not only a major label that created its own influential musical style, but one of the largest black-owned businesses in U.S. history.

Keeping a Loan Log

At times, you may need to double-check whether you actually made a previous payment (assuming you are managing your repayment yourself). For this purpose, you should create a record of your payments, often called a "loan log." While the repayment schedule tells you what you *should* do, the loan log is intended to document what you *actually* do.

Even if you've got a perfect memory, your lender may not. The loan log turns into an excellent tool for preserving the relationship between you and your lender, providing an immediate reference source if your lender believes you've missed a payment. The log also allows you to see how close you are to the finish line.

If others need to get involved in your affairs, a loan log will tell them the exact status of the loan. For example, if you or your lender were to die before the loan had been paid off, whoever was managing the estate would find the loan log very useful. It documents your progress in repaying the loan, allowing you, or your lender's estate administrator, to figure out the extent of the remaining obligation.

To create a loan log, set up a spreadsheet like the one below. A template is available in Appendix B, and on the Loan Forms CD at the back of this book. You can also use *Quicken* or *Quickbooks* since they have tools for managing installment payments (however, they do not automatically adjust amortized payments). You need to use an online calculator to do that and update the payment schedule manually.

Fill in the names of the lender and borrower, the original amount of the loan, and the date the loan was made at the top of the loan log. Record the following information in your loan log each time you make a payment:

- **Payment number.** Give each payment a number, from "1" through your last payment (normally corresponding to the payment numbers on your repayment schedule).
- **Payment due date.** In most cases, payments are due on the first of the month, but put whatever payment schedule is on your promissory note.

Loan Log

Name of Lender: _____

Name of Borrower: _____

Original Amount Borrowed: $_____

Date Loan Made: _____

Payment number	Payment due date	Total amount due	Payment paid date	Total amount paid	Principal paid	Interest paid	Late payment Date paid	Late fee	Evidence of payment	Other

- **Total amount due.** This is the total amount you owe on the payment.
- **Payment paid date.** Enter the date you actually send the check or make the payment.
- **Total amount paid.** This is the total amount for which you write the check or otherwise pay. If it isn't the amount listed on your repayment schedule, explain this in the far right column (Other).
- **Principal paid.** This amount will probably come directly from your repayment schedule. However, sometimes borrowers like to pay ahead or pay down either interest or principal. If you do this, you'll probably need to recalculate the repayment schedule.
- **Interest paid.** See "Principal paid," above.
- **Date paid late.** If you pay late, indicate the date.
- **Amount of late fee.** If your payment was late and you agreed to a late fee in your promissory note, note here how much you paid.

- **Evidence of payment.** If you paid with a check, write down the check number. If you're using a direct deposit system, examine your account and note the date the deposit went in. If, in the future, anyone questions whether or not you made a payment, this is the place where you should go to obtain that evidence.
- **Other.** If any other unusual circumstances arose or you and your lender verbally agreed to any change related to this particular payment, note these here. For example, if the lender forgave the payment knowing that you had a difficult month, mention that here.

You might recommend that your lender keep a loan log as well. The only difference from yours should be that your lender's log has a column for the dates when he or she receives your payments, as opposed to the dates when you sent them.

Acting Responsibly When You Can't Make a Payment

Cash flow crunches are not uncommon in the life of a small business. Perhaps a major customer cancels an order, the price of raw materials goes up dramatically, the economy takes a nose dive and the market for your product or service dries up, or you lose the day job that was helping you support your new venture. It's possible to weather both minor and major disasters—but not if you put your head in the sand and hope they go away. If you happen to hit a stretch where you have difficulty repaying, talk to your lender about ways to adjust the repayment schedule until you get back on your feet.

Once you've recognized that a cash flow crunch is looming, check your repayment schedule to see if you'll have a problem making your payments in full, on time. Communication is key: Whether you need a short-term or a long-term change in your loan agreement, talk to your lender. While no agreement can completely soften the blow of a missed payment, most entrepreneurs find that their friends and family would rather find out about cash flow problems early on than have you keep

Entrepreneur Finds the Limits of His Uncle's Flexibility

Dante had always wanted to take pictures for a living. After honing his photography skills and developing an impressive list of contacts, he finally put together a business plan and asked his Uncle Al to lend him $66,500.

Uncle Al agreed to a fairly generous loan: 0% interest, to be repaid on an amortized schedule (regular payments) over a term of five-and-a-half years. Payments on the principal-only loan worked out to just over $1,000 a month, and Dante launched his venture.

Unfortunately, the 9/11 attacks occurred just months later. Not only was the business community in shock, but the World Trade Towers were among the very landmarks that Dante had planned to use in his work.

Dante described for Uncle Al the difficulties in signing new clients, and the two agreed to cut Dante's payments in half for six months. They hoped that the market would start moving by then. After the six months passed, the loan reverted to the original payment plan of about $1,000 due each month.

Before long, Dante realized that he just couldn't keep up with that full payment, and he asked his uncle for another break. Uncle Al agreed to another six months of half payments. Dante made those payments; $500 seemed an amount he could handle. When the six months were up, he once again asked Uncle Al to agree to a half-payment schedule.

Uncle Al said no. He'd decided he couldn't let the wrangling continue and wanted a repayment schedule to which Dante would adhere. After a difficult conversation in which Uncle Al expressed feeling taken advantage of, and Dante faced up to the painful economic realities of his struggling business, the two came up with a plan. Dante would keep his business but do it on the side, and would take a new job allowing him to repay the $1,000 per month he owed on the loan.

As it turns out, Dante's paycheck from his new job arrives the day his loan payment is due each month, so that his loan repayment check arrives at his uncle's home within the seven-day allotted grace period. This is by no means the happy ending Dante had envisioned. But the private loan gave Dante a chance to get started and gave the pair the flexibility to make adjustments to handle the vagaries of Dante's business them a secret until the business goes under. Family and friend lenders' first instincts are usually to want to help you, perhaps by modifying the repayment schedule, before the problem becomes a crisis.

> **TIP**
> **Before talking to your lender, reread your promissory note.** It will tell you how you agreed to handle late or missed payments.

Although you may feel embarrassed to admit to your difficulties, you'll only look worse if your lender has to figure out him- or herself that your payment is late—leading the lender to believe that you're an irresponsible borrower. In addition, it's only considerate to let your lender know that a payment will not arrive when expected. Your lender may be counting on your payment to pay his or her own bills from the same bank account.

Depending on the severity of your cash crunch, you can use one of the following strategies when you can't make a full payment by your due date:

- Make the most of the grace period.
- Offer an alternative, such as a partial payment.
- Restructure the entire loan repayment schedule.

Making the Most of Your Grace Period

Double-check your promissory note to see whether it includes a grace period—that is, a preset number of days between when your loan payment is due and when it is considered overdue enough that you owe a late fee or are in default. Family and friend lenders tend to use grace periods of ten to 15 days. A grace period of ten calendar days, for example, means that although your payment may be due on the 1st of the month, you can't be penalized until after the 10th.

You can use your grace period to hold off making your loan payment until you have sufficient cash, if the timing is that close. Nevertheless, you should advise your lender that the payment won't be arriving on the due date.

> **CAUTION**
> **Don't abuse your grace period.** If you always make your payments on the last day of the grace period, you may give the impression that you are taking advantage of your lender. Make paying by your due date your habit, and use the grace period only when absolutely necessary.

Offering Your Lender an Alternative When Missing a Payment

If you are unable to make a payment one month—but don't yet believe the situation is critical enough to restructure the entire loan agreement—you and your lender can agree to one of several options. For example, you might skip a payment but make it up later (extending the loan term by one additional payment period). Or, your lender can agree that you'll spread out the payment across several subsequent payments. You'll have to calculate this—for example, by dividing your payment by ten and adding that amount to each of your next ten payments. Finally, your lender could forgive the payment entirely (nothing forces your lender to pursue any remedies at all).

These solutions do not require any changes to the original loan documents. But you should write up a brief description of the solution to your missed payment problem, sign it and have your lender do the same, and keep it with your records. If it's a matter of forgiving the whole loan (not just one payment), see Chapter 11, "When a Loan Turns Into a Gift: Creating a Loan Repayment Forgiveness Letter," for advice on doing this.

If, however, you find yourself on the phone with your lender every month or two requesting an alternative payment method, it may be time to think about completely restructuring your loan agreement.

Changing Your Repayment Schedule and Preparing a New Promissory Note

At a certain point, you may realize that your existing loan agreement just isn't realistic given the current state of your business or the market. For example, perhaps you're bringing in some revenue, but it's never quite enough to cover both your loan payments and your rent. Under such circumstances, you'll appreciate the flexibility of working with friends and family members. After all, their main goal is to help you succeed, not to tighten the screws and squeeze every dollar out of you by the due date.

If circumstances are causing you to regularly pay late or miss your payments altogether, perhaps a different payment schedule might work better. Most private lenders will be only too happy to negotiate such a change in your payment schedule if it means you can resume making regular payments. Of course, I'm not recommending you take advantage of your lender's willingness to be flexible. The object here is to come to an arrangement that ultimately allows you to pay the debt in full, not to wiggle out of your payment obligations.

When it comes to restructuring the loan, your options include:

- stretching out your payments over a longer term
- setting a longer interval between payments
- electing a lower interest rate, or
- switching to a different type of repayment plan (for example, one with different payments during busy and slow seasons).

The online loan calculators available at nolo.com and other sites will help you experiment with different types of payment schedules. Note that when you make changes to the terms of a loan that result in a new payment schedule, you need to draw up a new promissory note.

SEE AN EXPERT

Is there no chance that you can catch up or keep up with the repayment schedule in your promissory note? Your best bet may be to hire a professional to help you completely restructure your loan with a realistic payment schedule.

Changing the Loan Agreement When Profits Don't Meet Projections

Maria borrowed $10,000 from a friend to help launch her dream restaurant in Santa Fe, New Mexico. It was an upscale eatery featuring vegetarian Mexican food. Knowing that restaurants are expensive to start, and that it would take several months to earn enough to make significant loan payments, Maria and her friend negotiated a graduated loan with 5.5% interest, to be paid back over the course of three years. According to the schedule, in the first year, Maria would make monthly payments of $184; in the second year, her payments would increase to $316; and in the third and final year of the loan, she would pay $439 each month.

A few months into the second year, however, Maria realized that the restaurant's sales were not increasing as quickly as she had projected. Making the higher ($316) monthly payments was becoming a major problem.

Fortunately, Maria had been good about communicating with her friend/lender. She'd shared with her all the good news her first year of business had brought and felt comfortable talking with her about the loan. Maria sat down with her lender, showed her the numbers, and said that she feared that unless they restructured the loan she'd have to default. Her lender agreed with Maria's assessment, and the two calculated the remainder due on the loan, about $7,600, and set it up as a new loan.

The new agreement was for an amortized loan at a 7% interest rate for a term of nearly five years. (Maria chose the amortized structure because she specifically didn't want an increase in loan payments to sneak up on her.) This helped Maria by bringing the monthly payments down below $200. The higher interest rate, meanwhile, compensated the lender for the fact that she'd have to wait longer for the entire principal to be repaid.

This isn't the end of the story, however. Although Maria was doing well at making the monthly payments, she realized that the growing business needed new kitchen equipment—which would cost $40,000. Impressed at Maria's creativity in accessing flexible capital, her business partner, Ana, looked to her own circle of contacts. Ana didn't have to look far. Her father agreed to finance the purchase at 6% for three years. The restaurant now makes direct monthly payments of $1,216 into his bank account, as planned in their promissory note.

If You Have No Choice but to Default

Chances are that you'll ultimately find some way to repay your loan, so long as you communicate with your lender about cash difficulties and restructure the agreement as necessary. Default on a private loan is rare. But disaster can always strike—for example, if an irreplaceable business partner dies or your lender develops his or her own financial difficulties and can't be flexible about your loan.

> **SEE AN EXPERT**
>
> **A mediator can help you repair communications with your lender.** If you are resorting to default because you and your lender have stopped communicating about your difficulties repaying the loan, consider hiring a mediation service. It's far more cost-effective to pay a neutral third party to help you negotiate a restructured payment plan than to face the penalties of not paying your lender back at all. For more information on mediation and advice on finding a good mediator, see the Mediation FAQ at nolo.com.

According to the promissory note, once you have missed a payment, your lender has the right to initiate a collections process. Your lender, an attorney, or another professional may begin sending you a series of sternly worded letters demanding repayment. The culmination of this process is usually a report of your default to the national credit agencies. This could seriously damage your future ability to borrow funds from any institutional lender for either business or personal use.

Your lender has legal grounds on which to sue you if there is no other way to collect payment on the loan. If successful, the lender may get a court judgment for the amount owed plus court costs and possibly all or part of his or her attorney fees for obtaining the judgment. With a court judgment, the lender can then go after your assets.

Alternately, the lender can foreclose on the collateral you provided if the loan agreement included a security interest. Lawsuits and foreclosures are rare in private lending. Most family and friends would rather live with a bad-debt tax deduction than start litigation against someone they know.

The only silver lining to your default is that your lender will probably be able to claim the unpaid amount on his or her taxes as a nonbusiness bad debt. This is known as a short-term capital loss which lenders must report on an IRS tax form called Schedule D, *Capital Gains and Losses*. See "Bad-Debt Tax Deductions for Your Lender" in Chapter 3 for advice on making sure your lender can claim this deduction (if it becomes necessary). All the lender will need to do is write a letter to you demanding repayment, then a memo for his or her file stating that the loan is uncollectible. You may be able to help your lender successfully get this past the IRS by providing a financial statement showing your inability to pay your debts.

RESOURCE

Want more information on the rules and requirements for bad-debt tax deductions? See IRS Publication 550, *Investment Income and Expenses*, specifically the subsection of Chapter 4 called "Nonbusiness Bad Debts." It's available at the IRS website, www.irs.gov.

Handling Gifts From Family and Friends

FORMS ON CD-ROM

Chapter 11 includes instructions for, and samples of, the following forms, which are in Appendix B and on the Loan Forms CD included at the back of this book:

- Basic Gift Letter
- Loan Repayment Forgiveness Letter

Gifts of business capital, like other gifts, may come to you unexpectedly. You might be casually talking to a close relative or friend about launching your new business, only to have the person offer a gift of money to help you get started. If this hasn't yet happened to you, it may still be worth asking more directly for such a gift. In polite society, asking someone for a gift of money doesn't normally look too good—but when you're starting a business, it can make sense. Of course, you probably would only approach people whom you knew were already thinking of making you a gift, such as a grandparent or other well-off relative. For advice on approaching your parents or others for a cash gift, see earlier chapters, on preparing for and making your pitch for a loan, such as Chapter 5 which explains the value of developing a thought-out business plan.

Subway Sandwich Chain Began With Help From a Family Friend

When Fred DeLuca graduated from high school in the summer of 1965, his family didn't even have enough money to pay for college tuition. At a reunion barbecue, he asked a visiting older family friend, Dr. Buck, for advice. Dr. Buck suggested Fred open a sandwich shop, and they talked over how such a business would work. Later, as he was leaving, Dr. Buck wrote Fred a check for $1,000. Today, Subway lays claim to being the world's largest submarine sandwich chain, with more than 30,000 restaurants in 87 countries. (See the company history at www.subway.com.)

A gift is the simplest form of capital you can receive. It implies no ongoing obligation to the giver, other than your personal ethical obligation to thank the person and maintain good relations (as discussed in Chapter 10).

This chapter covers three basic issues involved with accepting a gift for your business:

- making sure that the amount of the gift falls within IRS limits for gifting

- documenting that the money is a gift (this is primarily for the giver who needs to keep a copy of a gift letter for tax purposes), and
- preparing the paperwork you need for turning a loan into a gift.

Dealing With IRS Limits on Gift Amounts

There's no such thing as a free lunch—or in this case, a free gift. Under current federal tax rules, someone who gives away more than $13,000 per year to any one person will be assessed a federal "gift tax" at the same rate as the estate tax. (It's the IRS's way of making sure people don't use gifts to avoid later estate tax payments.) Under IRS rules, you may receive up to $13,000 each year from any one person as a tax-free gift. This translates to $26,000 from a married couple, and if the gift is from your parents to you and your spouse, it increases to $52,000 ($13,000 from each individual to each individual).

If you receive less than $13,000 from someone, no one needs to report anything to the IRS. If you receive more than $13,000, the giver should file a gift tax return (IRS Form 709, *U.S. Gift Tax Return)* for the amount given over $13,000. Although the giver probably won't have to pay any tax for that particular year, the IRS will be keeping tabs on the giver's lifetime giving—the maximum is $1 million before taxes are owed. Even so, the giver's tax liability won't be settled until he or she dies and estate taxes are calculated.

A lender who wants to benefit from the gift tax exemption, must make the gift to you as an individual, since no exemption exists for business entities. Even if the gift is set up to be made to the business, the IRS will simply attribute it to the owner of the company. For example, if your uncle gives you $10,000 for a car and then another $10,000 for your new coffee shop in the same tax year, he will have made, in effect, a $20,000 gift to you. Since he has exceeded the annual gift tax exclusion, he will have to file a gift tax return so that the IRS can record the $7,000 (the amount over $13,000) against his lifetime exclusion from estate taxes.

RESOURCE

Looking for details on the annual gift tax exclusion? See the IRS website at www.irs.gov, in particular Publication 950, *Introduction to Estate and Gift Taxes.*

Make Sure Your Family Means "Gift" When They Say "Gift"

You'd think it would be easy to communicate what is a loan and what is a gift. But when you look at how real families operate, the lines are often surprisingly blurry. Take the case of Ernie, whose parents had been giving him a so-called "gift" of around $20,000 annually (depending on the then-current gift-tax exclusion) since he was a teenager. This money was kept in a separate bank account in Ernie's name, but here's the catch: It was not to be touched by Ernie without his parents' permission. When Ernie entered business school, they mutually agreed that Ernie could use the money for school expenses, but that Ernie would have to pay back to the account anything he withdrew.

Just a few years later, Ernie had graduated from business school, owed about $70,000 to the account, and was planning a wedding with his fiancée, herself recently out of grad school. Neither had enough money saved up for the dream wedding both wanted (which would cost about $18,000). Ernie by now had developed a sense of entitlement to the money, legally in his name. He did intend to repay the education loan to the account but also wanted to use some to fund the wedding.

However, Ernie's parents remained firm that the money could be used only for education, real estate, or other asset-building opportunities. After months of tension, the family compromised. They decided that Ernie could withdraw up to $10,000 of the remaining funds in the account for the wedding, as an out-and-out gift. But if Ernie wanted to use any more for the wedding, or as living expenses until the pair settled into new jobs, it would have be as a loan, to be repaid to the account.

Why You Need—And How to Get—A Gift Letter

For tax and other reasons (described in Chapter 8), even an outright gift (like a loan) needs to be supported by some written documentation. Gift letters typically take two forms, either:

- a basic letter documenting a one-time gift to the individual, or
- a loan repayment forgiveness letter (discussed below), documenting that a certain payment or group of payments once due to a lender under a loan agreement is now to be considered a gift.

When someone intends to transfer money as a gift, not a loan or investment, he or she needs to write a letter to the recipient explaining this. The letter should specify the amount of the gift, and explicitly say that the money is meant as a gift and that the giver does not expect to be repaid. This is a very simple letter that you or the giver can draft at home. It doesn't need to be notarized to be valid.

Below is a sample letter that Kalah drafted for her grandfather Marcus to sign when he gave her $9,000 to help launch her children's bookstore, Hobby Horse Books. Use this gift letter as a sample (a template is available in Appendix B and on the Loan Forms CD at the back of this book).

Basic Gift Letter

Kalah Brown
123 Main Street
Princeton, NJ 08540

To Kalah:

By my signature below, I hereby gift $9,000 to my granddaughter Kalah Brown to use as she wishes. I expect no repayment or services in return for this gift.

Marcus Brown
Marcus Brown

Date: December 1, 2009

When a Loan Turns Into a Gift: Creating a Loan Repayment Forgiveness Letter

If a money transfer starts out as a loan, a generous lender can easily turn part or all of it into a gift, simply by saying, "No need to repay it after all." Of course, you'll want to get this in writing, for tax and other financial reasons. To do this, you'll need what's called a "loan payment forgiveness letter."

This letter can be short, simply identifying the loan and stating the originally agreed-upon repayment amount and due date, then expressing the lender's forgiveness of all or some of that repayment. Here's a (simplistic) example: Sydney signs a promissory note promising to pay Jan $10,000, making annual payments of $2,000 over a five-year period. A year into the loan, Jan decides to forgive Sydney that year's payment of $2,000. To forgive this payment, Jan would send Sydney a loan payment forgiveness letter, such as the one show below.

Use this letter as a sample in preparing your own—for example, if your lender is forgiving you one monthly payment, you would use the term "Monthly Payment," not "Annual Payment." (A template is available in Appendix B and on the Loan Forms CD at the back of this book.) The lender must sign the letter, give the original to you (the borrower), and keep a copy for tax records. The lender will also need to include a copy with his or her annual tax paperwork.

CAUTION

Be careful. If someone starts out intending to forgive loan payments, then the transaction is not really a loan—it's a gift. And if it's large enough—currently, more than $13,000 to one recipient in a calendar year—the giver is required by law to file a federal gift tax return. Talk to a knowledgeable lawyer if large sums are involved.

Sample Loan Repayment Forgiveness Letter

Sydney Springer
15 Grove Street
Berkeley, CA 94709

To Sydney:

I made a loan of $10,000 to you on February 15, 2009. Under the terms of our promissory note, this loan has a payment ("Annual Payment") of $2,000 due to me on February 15, 2010.

By my signature below, I forgive all of this Annual Payment.

By signing this notice, I do not waive the right to choose to receive any subsequent Annual Payments under the promissory note you signed on February 15, 2009.

Jan Springer
Jan Springer
229 Oceanview
Berkeley, CA 94707

Date: January 1, 2010

This is a very straightforward way that someone would use a loan repayment forgiveness letter. There are also more complex uses of this type of letter. Someone who wants to give you more than $13,000 in a single year (the IRS limit on annual gift amounts) without using up any of the lifetime exclusion of $1 million, may try to achieve this by structuring the transfer as a loan, with repayments due periodically over a number of years. Your lender then has the option to receive or forgive payments as they come due. The lender does this by picking financial terms that result in no more than $13,000 in payments due over the course of any one year. Then, each year, your lender must send you a loan forgiveness letter stating that all payments scheduled for that year are forgiven. Your attorneys may, however, advise you, the borrower, to make a few payments each year, so as to create a repayment paper trail.

EXAMPLE: Emil's best friend Juan, who happens to be a millionaire, gives Emil $30,000 with which to start a printing and engraving business. However, Juan wishes to both make a gift and avoid exceeding his annual gift tax liability. After consulting with his accountant, Juan asks Emil to write a promissory note saying that he'll repay the loan with a repayment plan that includes quarterly payments each year for three years. Each year, Emil makes his first quarterly payment, but then, before the 2nd, 3rd, and 4th quarter payments come due, Juan sends him letters declaring that the next payment is to be forgiven. In this way, Emil gets a substantial gift from Juan, and Juan does not exceed his annual gifting exemption with the IRS.

If you enter into a loan agreement knowing that your lender will probably forgive some or all of the payments (for tax reasons, some lenders may prefer structuring the initial transfer of funds as a loan), it makes sense to set up the loan with annual or quarterly payments. This saves the lender from sending monthly loan forgiveness letters—a task that might make any lender feel a lot less forgiving. Remember, if the amount the lender wants to forgive each year is higher than $13,000, the lender may exceed his or her annual gift tax exemption. Have your lender consult with a tax adviser about any concerns regarding how the IRS may perceive your particular arrangement.

For example, if Kalah's grandfather Marcus had wanted to provide $30,000 (not $9,000 per the example above) to help launch her bookstore, but wanted to do it without exceeding his annual gift tax exemption, the pair could have set up a loan for three years with annual payments of $13,000 or less. Then, each year, Kalah's grandfather could have sent her a letter like the one above, forgiving the payments when they came due.

How to Use the CD-ROM

The CD-ROM included with this book can be used with Windows computers. It installs files that use software programs that need to be on your computer already. It is not a stand-alone software program.

In accordance with U.S. copyright laws, the CD-ROM and its files are for your personal use only.

Two types of files are included:

- word processing (RTF) files that you can open, complete, print, and save with your word processing program (see "Using the Word Processing Files to Create Documents," below), and
- a Portable Document Format (PDF) file that can be viewed only with Adobe *Reader* (see "Using the Print-Only File," below). This file is designed to be filled in and printed out, but filled-in versions cannot be saved.

See the end of this appendix for a list of files, their file names, and their file formats.

Please read this appendix and the "Readme.htm" file included on the CD-ROM for instructions on using the CD-ROM.

How to View the README File

To view the "Readme.htm" file, insert the CD-ROM into your computer's CD-ROM drive and follow these instructions:

Windows XP and Vista

1. On your PC's desktop, double-click the **My Computer** icon.

2. Double-click the icon for the CD-ROM drive into which the CD-ROM was inserted.

3. Double-click the file "Readme.htm."

Macintosh

1. On your Mac desktop, double-click the icon for the CD-ROM that you inserted.

2. Double-click the file "Readme.htm."

Note to Macintosh users: This CD-ROM and its files should also work on Macintosh computers. Please note, however, that Nolo cannot provide technical support for non-Windows users.

Note to eBook users: You can access the CD files mentioned here from the bookmarked section of the eBook, located on the lefthand side.

Installing the Files Onto Your Computer

To work with the files on the CD-ROM, you first need to install them onto your hard disk. Here's how.

Windows XP and Vista

Follow the CD-ROM's instructions that appear on the screen.
  If nothing happens when you insert the CD-ROM, then:
1. Double-click the **My Computer** icon.
2. Double-click the icon for the CD-ROM drive into which the CD-ROM was inserted.
3. Double-click the file "Setup.exe."

Macintosh

If the **Loan Forms CD** window is not open, double-click the **Loan Forms CD** icon. Then:
1. Select the **Loan Forms** folder icon.
2. Drag and drop the folder icon onto your computer.

Where Are the Files Installed?

Windows

By default, all the files are installed to the **Loan Forms** folder in the **Program Files** folder of your computer and added to the **Programs** folder of the **Start** menu.

Macintosh

All the files are located in the **Loan Forms** folder.

Using the Word Processing Files to Create Documents

The CD-ROM includes word processing files that you can open, complete, print, and save with your word processing program. All word processing files come in Rich Text Format and have the extension ".rtf." For example, the file for the Best Bets List discussed in Chapter 4 is on the file "BestBetsList.rtf." RTF files can be read by most recent word processing programs including Microsoft *Word*, Windows *WordPad*, and recent versions of *WordPerfect*.

The following are general instructions. Because each word processor uses different commands to open, format, save, and print documents, refer to your word processor's help file for specific instructions.

Do not call Nolo's technical support if you have questions on how to use your word processor or your computer.

Opening a File

You can open word processing files with any of the three following ways:

1. Windows users can open a file by selecting its "shortcut:"
   - Click the Windows **Start** button.
   - Open the **Programs** folder.
   - Open The **Loan Forms** folder.
   - Click the shortcut to the file you want to work with.
2. Both Windows and Macintosh users can open a file by double-clicking it:
   - Use **My Computer** or **Windows Explorer** (Windows XP or Vista) or the **Finder** (Macintosh) to go to the **Loan Forms** folder.
   - Double-click the file you want to open.
3. Windows and Macintosh users can open a file from within their word processors:
   - Open your word processor.
   - Go to the **File** menu and choose the **Open** command. This opens a dialog box where you select the location and name of

the file. (Navigate to the version of the **Loan Forms** folder that you've installed on your computer.)

Editing Your Document

Here are tips for working on your document:

- Refer to the book's instructions and sample agreements for help.
- Underlines indicate where to enter information, frequently including bracketed instructions. Delete the underlines and instructions before finishing your document.
- Signature lines should appear on a page with at least some text from the document itself.

Editing Files That Have Optional or Alternative Text

Some files have optional or alternate text:

- With optional text, you choose whether to include or exclude the given text.
- With alternative text, you select one alternative to include and exclude the other alternatives.

When editing these files, we suggest you do the following:

Optional text

Delete optional text you do not want to include and keep that which you do want. In either case, delete the italicized instructions. If you choose to delete an optional numbered clause, renumber the subsequent clauses after deleting it.

Alternative text

First, delete all the alternatives that you do not want to include. Then, delete the italicized instructions.

Printing Out the Document

Use your word processor's or text editor's **Print** command to print out your document.

Saving Your Document

Use the **Save As** command to save and rename your document. You will be unable to use the **Save** command because the files are "read-only." If you save the file without renaming it, the underlines that indicate where you need to enter your information will be lost, and you will be unable to create a new document with this file without recopying the original file from the CD-ROM.

Using the Print-Only File

The CD-ROM includes a useful file in Adobe PDF format. To use it, you need to have installed on your computer Adobe *Reader*, which you can download for free at www.adobe.com.

Opening the PDF File

The PDF file, like the word processing files, can be opened in one of three ways:

1. Windows users can open a file by selecting its "shortcut":
   - Click the Windows **Start** button.
   - Open the **Programs** folder.
   - Open the **Loan Forms** folder.
   - Double-click the shortcut to the file you want to work with.
2. Both Windows and Macintosh users can open a file directly by double-clicking it:
   - Use **My Computer** or **Windows Explorer** (Windows XP or Vista) or the **Finder** (Macintosh) to go to the **Loan Forms** folder.
   - Double-click the specific file you want to open.
3. Windows and Macintosh users can open a file from within Adobe *Reader*.
   - Open Adobe *Reader*.
   - Go to the **File** menu and choose the **Open** command. This opens a dialog box where you select the location and name of the file. (Navigate to the version of the **Loan Forms** folder that you've installed on your computer.)

Filling in PDF files

The PDF file can be filled out using your computer, but you will be unable to save the filled-in version. You will, however, be able to print it out.

Files on the CD-ROM

The following files are in Rich Text Format (RTF):

Form Title	File Name
Best Bets List	BestBetsList.rtf
Start-Up Costs Worksheet	StartUpCosts.rtf
Recurring Costs Worksheet	RecurringCost.rtf
Collateral List	CollateralList.rtf
Loan Request Letter	LoanRequest.rtf
Gift Letter: Basic	GiftBasic.rtf
Gift Letter: Loan Repayment Forgiveness	ForgivenessLetter.rtf
Promissory Note (for an amortized loan)	PromissoryAmortized.rtf
Promissory Note (for a graduated loan)	PromissoryGraduated.rtf
Promissory Note (for a seasonal loan)	PromissorySeasonal.rtf
Promissory Note (for an interest-only loan)	PromissoryInterest.rtf
Promissory Note Modifications for a Loan to a Business	ModBusiness.rtf
Promissory Note Modifications for Signature by Notary Public	ModNotary.rtf
Security Agreement	SecurityAgreement.rtf
Loan Log	LoanLog.rtf

The following file is in Adobe Portable Document Format (PDF):

Form Title	File Name
UCC Financing Statement and Instructions	UCC1.pdf

Small Business Loans Forms and Worksheets

Name of form	Discussed in Chapter	File name
Best Bets List	4	BestBetsList.rtf
Start-Up Costs Worksheet	5	StartUpCosts.rtf
Recurring Costs Worksheet	5	RecurringCost.rtf
Collateral List	6	CollateralList.rtf
Loan Request Letter	7	LoanRequest.rtf
Promissory Note (for an amortized loan)	9	PromissoryAmortized.rtf
Promissory Note (for a graduated loan)	9	PromissoryGraduated.rtf
Promissory Note (for a seasonal loan)	9	PromissorySeasonal.rtf
Promissory Note (for an interest-only loan)	9	PromissoryInterest.rtf
Promissory Note Modifications for a Loan to a Business	9	ModBusiness.rtf
Promissory Note Modifications for Signature by Notary Public	9	ModNotary.rtf
Security Agreement	9	SecurityAgreement.rtf
UCC Financing Statement	9	UCC1.pdf
Loan Log	10	LoanLog.rtf
Gift Letter: Basic	11	GiftBasic.rtf
Gift Letter: Loan Repayment Forgiveness	11	ForgivenessLetter.rtf

Best Bets List

Prospect Name	Prospect Description	Contact Information	Amount to Request

Start-Up Costs Worksheet

Description	Estimated cost
Legal fees	$
Rent (include deposit and first month)	$
Office equipment	$
Insurance (initial premium)	$
Business license	$
Stationery, logos, letterhead	$
Initial advertising	$
Other	$
Total start-up costs	$

Recurring Costs Worksheet

Description	Estimated monthly cost
Monthly rent	$
Payroll	$
Utilities	$
Insurance	$
Ongoing advertising	$
Association and other memberships	$
Other	$
Total monthly recurring costs	$

Collateral List

Item Description   **Approximate Value**

Business Assets

_____ $ _____

_____ $ _____

_____ $ _____

_____ $ _____

_____ $ _____

_____ $ _____

_____ $ _____

_____ $ _____

_____ $ _____

_____ $ _____

_____ $ _____

_____ $ _____

Personal Assets

_____ $ _____

_____ $ _____

_____ $ _____

_____ $ _____

_____ $ _____

_____ $ _____

_____ $ _____

_____ $ _____

_____ $ _____

_____ $ _____

Loan Request Letter

[*date*] _____

[*address line 1*] _____

[*address line 2*] _____

[*address line 3*] _____

Dear Friend and Supporter,

I am excited to tell you about a way for you to support [*business name*] and earn an attractive return. [*Business name*] is raising $[*total loan amount*] from relatives, friends, and business associates, and I thought you might be interested in participating. [*Optional:* Attached to this letter are [*number of*] loan options for you to consider; the loan amount and interest rate varies with each.]

[*Optional:* I've already raised $[*amount*] from family members and from [*awards or other sources*]. I thought you might be interested in providing a loan for the remaining $[*amount*].]

[*Write one or two paragraphs here describing the highlights of your business, for example, what you will sell, who will buy it, why they'll buy it, and why now is the right time. Refer to an attached business plan or executive summary, if provided.*]

I offer you this opportunity because I believe it is good for my business and good for you. For me, it allows me to raise the money I need to grow my business from people I trust, and at an affordable rate. For you, the [*interest rate*]% I'm offering provides a competitive short-term return on your money. If you choose to make the loan, [*summarize repayment plan*].

[*Choose one of the next two options*]

[*Option 1*] In addition, my proposal offers you the protection of a legally binding loan agreement. If you agree to the loan terms set forth in this letter, I'll prepare a promissory note reflecting my promise to repay the loan at these terms. The loan will start on the day we transfer the funds. I'll send a check from my business account to the address you specify, will maintain a loan log of my payments, and will have my accountant provide you year-end tax summary reports.

[OR]

[Option 2] In addition, my proposal offers you the protection of a legally binding loan agreement and the convenience of a third party to manage the repayment. I have retained [name and description of third party] to handle our loan. [Name of third party] has created a promissory note for us and will manage the repayment of the loan. My repayments to you will be preauthorized to come out of the [business name] corporate account electronically, and the funds will be deposited into a bank account that you designate. [Name of third party] will also provide us access to information about payment status history, maintain records, and provide year-end tax summary reports.

[End of Options]

I hope that you will consider this mutually beneficial opportunity. I truly believe that [business name] is poised for success and I look forward to your support in growing the business. Thank you for your consideration; I look forward to discussing this opportunity with you further.

Sincerely,

_____

[signature]

_____

[name]

_____

[title]

_____

[business name]

Promissory Note (for an amortized loan)

1. **For Value Received,** [*borrower name*] ("Borrower") promises to pay to the order of [*lender name*], of [*city, state*] ("Lender"), the sum, in United States dollars, of [*amount of loan, spelled out*] dollars, ($_____), plus interest accruing at an annual rate of [*interest rate, spelled out*] percent (____%) on the unpaid principal amount beginning on [*loan start month/day/year*] (the "Debt").

2. **Transferability.** Borrower understands that the Lender may transfer this Note. The Lender or anyone who takes this Note by transfer and who is entitled to receive payments under this Note is called the "Note Holder" and will have the same rights and remedies as the Lender under this Note.

3. **Payments.** Payment of the Debt shall be made in [*monthly, quarterly, or annual*] installments by: [*choose one*]

   ☐ personal check sent to [*address where check is to be mailed*]

   ☐ direct deposit to [*institution and account number where deposit is to be made*]

   ☐ [*describe other form of payment*].

   Payments shall include principal and interest, as follows:

   Beginning on [*loan start date*] and continuing [*monthly, quarterly, or annually*] on the [*for example, 1st or 15th*] day of each [*month, quarter, or year*] (the "Due Date") until [*month/day/year of last payment*] (the "Final Due Date"), Borrower shall pay to the Lender or Note Holder the sum of $_____ each [*month, quarter, or year*] (the "[*Monthly, Quarterly, or Annual*] Payment"). On the Final Due Date, Borrower shall pay all amounts remaining due under the terms of this Note.

   [*Name of schedule*] lays out the payment schedule for this Note.

4. **Grace Period and Late Fee.** If the Borrower fails to make any payment in the full amount and within [*number of days spelled out*]

([*number in figures*]) calendar days (the "Grace Period") after the date it is due, Borrower agrees to pay a late charge to the Lender or Note Holder in the amount of $_____ (the "Late Fee"). Borrower will pay this Late Fee promptly but only once on each late payment.

5. **Security.** [*choose one*]

   ☐ This is an unsecured note.

   ☐ Borrower agrees that until this Note is paid in full (including principal and interest, if any), this Note will be secured by a separate security agreement (incorporated here as Attachment [*fill in*]), and, if applicable, a Uniform Commercial Code Financing Statement, giving Lender a security interest in the following property: [*describe asset*]_____

   _____ .

6. **Default and Acceleration.** If any installment payment due under this Note is not received by Lender within the Grace Period, the note will be in default and the entire amount of unpaid principal will become immediately due and payable at the option of Lender without prior notice of default to Borrower.

7. **Prepayment.** This Note may be prepaid in full at any time without cost or penalty to the Borrower.

8. **Attorneys' Fees.** If Lender prevails in a lawsuit to collect on this note, Borrower agrees to pay Lender's attorneys' fees in an amount the court finds to be just and reasonable.

9. **Waiver.** The undersigned and all other parties to this Note waive the following requirements:

   • presentment of the Note for payment by Lender
   • refusal of payment by Borrower after presentment of the Note by Lender, otherwise known as dishonor, and
   • Lender's notification to Borrower of Borrower's refusal to pay.

10. **Lender's Rights.** Lender's decision not to exercise a right or remedy under this Note at a given time does not waive the Lender's ability to exercise that right or remedy at a later date.

11. **Liability of Individual Borrowers.** The term "Borrower" may refer to one or more borrowers. If there is more than one borrower, they agree to be jointly and severally liable.

12. **Governing Law.** This agreement will be governed by and construed in accordance with the laws of the state of _____ .

Borrower's signature: _____

Print name: _____

Address: _____

_____

Date: _____

Promissory Note (for a graduated loan)

1. **For Value Received,** [*borrower name*] ("Borrower") promises to pay to the order of [*lender name*], of [*city, state*] ("Lender"), the sum, in United States dollars, of [*amount of loan, spelled out*] dollars ($_____), plus interest accruing at an annual rate of [*interest rate, spelled out*] percent (_____%) on the unpaid principal amount beginning on [*loan start month/day/year*] (the "Debt").

2. **Transferability.** Borrower understands that the Lender may transfer this Note. The Lender or anyone who takes this Note by transfer and who is entitled to receive payments under this Note is called the "Note Holder" and will have the same rights and remedies as the Lender under this Note.

3. **Payments.** Payment of the Debt shall be made in [monthly, quarterly, or annual] installments by: [*choose one*]

   ☐ personal check sent to [*address where check is to be mailed*]

   ☐ direct deposit to [*institution and account number where deposit is to be made*]

   ☐ [*describe other form of payment*].

   Payments shall include principal and interest, as follows:

   Beginning on [*repayment start month/day/year*] and continuing [monthly, quarterly, or annually] on the [*for example, 1st or 15th*] day of each [*month, quarter*, or year] through [*repayment end month/day/year (for first step)*], Borrower shall pay to lender the sum of $_____ .

   Beginning on [*repayment start date of next step*] and continuing [monthly, quarterly, or annually] on the [*for example, 1st or 15th*] day of each [*month, quarter*, or year] through [*repayment end date of next step*], Borrower shall pay to lender the sum of $_____ .

   Then, beginning on [*repayment start date of next step*] and continuing [monthly, quarterly, or annually] on the [*for example, 1st or 15th*] day of each [*month, quarter*, or year] through [*repayment *end date of next step*], Borrower shall pay to lender the sum of $_____ .

[*Insert additional sections as needed for additional steps of the loan*]

Finally, beginning on [*repayment start date of last step*] and continuing [monthly, quarterly, *or* annually] on the [*for example, 1st or 15th*] day of each [*month, quarter, or year*] until [*final payment date*], Borrower shall pay to lender the sum of $_____ .

On [*final due date (month/day/year)*], Borrower shall pay all amounts remaining due under the terms of this Note.

[*Name of schedule*] lays out the payment schedule for this Note.

4. **Grace Period and Late Fee.** If the Borrower fails to make any payment in the full amount and within [*number of days, spelled out*] ([*number in figures*]) calendar days (the "Grace Period") after the date it is due, Borrower agrees to pay a late charge to the Lender or Note Holder in the amount of $_____ (the "Late Fee"). Borrower will pay this Late Fee promptly but only once on each late payment.

5. **Security.** [*choose one*]

   ☐ This is an unsecured note.

   ☐ Borrower agrees that until this Note is paid in full (including principal and interest, if any), this Note will be secured by a separate security agreement (incorporated here as Attachment ([*fill in*]), and, if applicable, a Uniform Commercial Code Financing Statement, giving Lender a security interest in the following property: [*describe asset*] _____

   _____ .

6. **Default and Acceleration.** If any installment payment due under this Note is not received by Lender within the Grace Period, the note will be in default and the entire amount of unpaid principal will become immediately due and payable at the option of Lender without prior notice of default to Borrower.

7. **Prepayment.** This Note may be prepaid in full at any time without cost or penalty to the Borrower.

8. **Attorneys' Fees.** If Lender prevails in a lawsuit to collect on this note, Borrower agrees to pay Lender's attorneys' fees in an amount the court finds to be just and reasonable.

9. **Waiver.** The undersigned and all other parties to this Note waive the following requirements:
   - presentment of the Note for payment by Lender
   - refusal of payment by Borrower after presentment of the Note by Lender, otherwise known as dishonor, and
   - Lender's notification to Borrower of Borrower's refusal to pay.

10. **Lender's Rights.** Lender's decision not to exercise a right or remedy under this Note at a given time does not waive the Lender's ability to exercise that right or remedy at a later date.

11. **Liability of Individual Borrowers.** The term "Borrower" may refer to one or more borrowers. If there is more than one borrower, they agree to be jointly and severally liable.

12. **Governing Law.** This agreement will be governed by and construed in accordance with the laws of the state of _____ .

Borrower's signature: _____

Print name: _____

Address: _____

_____

Date: _____

Promissory Note (for a seasonal loan)

1. **For Value Received,** [*borrower name*] ("Borrower") promises to pay to the order of [*lender name*], of [*city, state*] ("Lender"), the sum, in United States dollars, of [*amount of loan, spelled out*] dollars ($_____), plus interest accruing at an annual rate of [*interest rate, spelled out*] percent (____%) on the unpaid principal amount beginning on [*loan start month/day/year*] (the "Debt").

2. **Transferability.** Borrower understands that the Lender may transfer this Note. The Lender or anyone who takes this Note by Transfer and who is entitled to receive payments under this Note is called the "Note Holder" and will have the same rights and remedies as the Lender under this Note.

3. **Payments.** Payment of the Debt shall be made in [monthly, quarterly, or annual] installments by: [*choose one*]

   ☐ personal check sent to [*address where check is to be mailed*]

   ☐ direct deposit to [*institution and account number where deposit is to be made*]

   ☐ [*describe other form of payment*].

   Payments shall include principal and interest, as follows:

   Beginning on [*repayment start month/day/year*] and continuing until [*month/day/year of final due date*], Borrower shall make monthly payments as described below:

   For the calendar months of [*list months of high season*] of each year, Borrower shall pay on the [*for example, 1st or 15th*] day of each month the sum of $ [*high-season payment amount*] to the Lender or Note Holder ("High-Season Monthly Payment").

   For the calendar months of [*list months of low season*] of each year, Borrower shall pay on the [*for example, 1st or 15th*] day of each month the sum of $ [*low-season payment amount*] to the Lender or Note Holder ("Low-Season Monthly Payment").

Finally, on [*month/day/year of final due date*], Borrower shall pay all amounts remaining due under the terms of this Note.

[*Name of schedule*] lays out the payment schedule for this Note.

4. **Grace Period and Late Fee.** If the Borrower fails to make any payment in the full amount and within [*number of days, spelled out*] ([*number in figures*]) calendar days (the "Grace Period") after the date it is due, Borrower agrees to pay a late charge to the Lender or Note Holder in the amount of $_____ (the "Late Fee"). Borrower will pay this Late Fee promptly but only once on each late payment.

5. **Security.** [*choose one*]
   ☐ This is an unsecured note.
   ☐ Borrower agrees that until this Note is paid in full (including principal and interest, if any), this Note will be secured by a separate security agreement (incorporated here as Attachment ([*fill in*]), and, if applicable, a Uniform Commercial Code Financing Statement, giving Lender a security interest in the following property: [*describe asset*] _____

   _____ .

6. **Default and Acceleration.** If any installment payment due under this Note is not received by Lender within the Grace Period, the note will be in default and the entire amount of unpaid principal will become immediately due and payable at the option of Lender without prior notice of default to Borrower.

7. **Prepayment.** This Note may be prepaid in full at any time without cost or penalty to the Borrower.

8. **Attorneys' Fees.** If Lender prevails in a lawsuit to collect on this note, Borrower agrees to pay Lender's attorneys' fees in an amount the court finds to be just and reasonable.

9. **Waiver.** The undersigned and all other parties to this Note waive the following requirements:
   • presentment of the Note for payment by Lender

- refusal of payment by Borrower after presentment of the Note by Lender, otherwise known as dishonor, and
- Lender's notification to Borrower of Borrower's refusal to pay.

10. **Lender's Rights.** Lender's decision not to exercise a right or remedy under this Note at a given time does not waive the Lender's ability to exercise that right or remedy at a later date.

11. **Liability of Individual Borrowers.** The term "Borrower" may refer to one or more borrowers. If there is more than one borrower, they agree to be jointly and severally liable.

12. **Governing Law.** This agreement will be governed by and construed in accordance with the laws of the state of _____ .

Borrower's signature: _____

Print name: _____

Address: _____

_____

Date: _____

Promissory Note (for an interest-only loan)

1. **For Value Received,** [*borrower name*] ("Borrower") promises to pay to the order of [*lender name*], of [*city, state*] ("Lender"), the sum, in United States dollars, of [*amount of loan, spelled out*] dollars ($_____), plus interest accruing at an annual rate of [*interest rate, spelled out*] percent (____%) on the unpaid principal amount beginning on [*loan start month/day/year*] (the "Debt").

2. **Transferability.** Borrower understands that the Lender may transfer this Note. The Lender or anyone who takes this Note by transfer and who is entitled to receive payments under this Note is called the "Note Holder" and will have the same rights and remedies as the Lender under this Note.

3. **Payments.** Payment of the Debt shall be made in [monthly, quarterly, or annual] installments by: [*choose one*]

   ☐ personal check sent to [*address where check is to be mailed*]

   ☐ direct deposit to [*institution and account number where deposit is to be made*]

   ☐ [*describe other form of payment*].

   Payments shall include principal and interest, as follows:

   Borrower will pay all interest that accrues during the term of the loan by making a payment every [month, quarter, or year]. Borrower will make [monthly, quarterly, or annual] payments on the [*for example, 1st or 15th*] day of each [month, quarter, or year] beginning on [*loan repayment start month/day/year*]. Borrower will make these payments every [month, quarter, or year] until Borrower has paid all of the interest and any other charges described below that Borrower may owe under this Note. Each payment will be applied as of its scheduled due date and will be applied to interest before principal.

On [*month/day/year of final due date*], Borrower will pay all remaining principal, interest, and any other amounts due to Lender under the terms of this Note.

[*Name of schedule*] lays out the payment schedule for this Note.

4. **Grace Period and Late Fee.** If the Borrower fails to make any payment in the full amount and within [*number of days, spelled out*] ([*number in figures*]) calendar days (the "Grace Period") after the date it is due, Borrower agrees to pay a late charge to the Lender or Note Holder in the amount of $_____ (the "Late Fee"). Borrower will pay this Late Fee promptly but only once on each late payment.

5. **Security.** [*choose one*]
   ☐ This is an unsecured note.
   ☐ Borrower agrees that until this Note is paid in full (including principal and interest, if any), this Note will be secured by a separate security agreement (incorporated here as Attachment [*fill in*]), and, if applicable, a Uniform Commercial Code Financing Statement, giving Lender a security interest in the following property: [*describe asset*] _____

   _____ .

6. **Default and Acceleration.** If any installment payment due under this Note is not received by Lender within the Grace Period, the note will be in default and the entire amount of unpaid principal will become immediately due and payable at the option of Lender without prior notice of default to Borrower.

7. **Prepayment.** This Note may be prepaid in full at any time without cost or penalty to the Borrower.

8. **Attorneys' Fees.** If Lender prevails in a lawsuit to collect on this note, Borrower agrees to pay Lender's attorneys' fees in an amount the court finds to be just and reasonable.

9. **Waiver.** The undersigned and all other parties to this Note waive the following requirements:

- presentment of the Note for payment by Lender
- refusal of payment by Borrower after presentment of the Note by Lender, otherwise known as dishonor, and
- Lender's notification to Borrower of Borrower's refusal to pay.

10. **Lender's Rights.** Lender's decision not to exercise a right or remedy under this Note at a given time does not waive the Lender's ability to exercise that right or remedy at a later date.

11. **Liability of Individual Borrowers.** The term "Borrower" may refer to one or more borrowers. If there is more than one borrower, they agree to be jointly and severally liable.

12. **Governing Law.** This agreement will be governed by and construed in accordance with the laws of the state of _____ .

Borrower's signature: _____

Print name: _____

Address: _____

_____

Date: _____

Promissory Note Modifications for a Loan to a Business

At the beginning, replace opening lines with the following:

For Value Received, [*name of your business*], a [*the U.S. state where your business was formed*] [*choose one:* corporation/partnership/LLC] with its principal place of business in [*city, state of business*] ("Borrower"), promises to pay ....

At the end, replace the signature block with the following:

Borrower: ___ [*print business name*] _____

By: __[*signature*]_____

Print name: _____

Title: _____

Address: _____

_____

Dated: _____

Promissory Note Modifications for Signature by Notary Public

Add the following to the end of your promissory note, after the signature block, if you plan to have a notary public witness the signing.

Certificate of Acknowledgment of Notary Public

State of _____

County of _____

On _____, before me, _____

_____, a notary public in and for said state,

personally appeared _____, who proved to me on the basis of satisfactory evidence to be the person whose name is subscribed to the within instrument and acknowledged to me that he or she executed the same in his or her authorized capacity and that by his or her signature on the instrument, the person, or the entity upon behalf of which the person acted, executed the instrument.

WITNESS my hand and official seal.

_____

Notary Public for the State of _____

My commission expires _____

[NOTARY SEAL]

Security Agreement

Name of Borrower: _____

Name of Lender: _____

1. **Grant of Security Interest.** Borrower grants to Lender a continuing security interest in the following personal property: _____

_____

_____

(the Secured Property). Borrower grants this security interest to secure performance of the promissory note dated _____ that Borrower executed in favor of Lender (the Note), which obligates Borrower to pay Lender $ _____ with interest at the rate of _____% per year, on the terms stated in the Note.

2. **Financing Statement.** Until the amount due under the Note is paid in full, the Note will be further secured by a Uniform Commercial Code (UCC) Financing Statement. Borrower agrees to sign any other documents that Lender reasonably requests to protect Lender's security interest in the Secured Property.

3. **Use and Care of Secured Property.** Until the amount due under the Note is paid in full, Borrower agrees to:
   A. maintain the Secured Property in good repair
   B. not sell, transfer, or release the Secured Property without Lender's prior written consent
   C. pay all taxes on the Secured Property as they become due, and
   D. allow Lender to inspect the Secured Property at any reasonable time.

4. **Borrower's Default.** If Borrower is more than _____ days late in making any payment due under the Note, or if Buyer fails to correct any violations of Paragraph 3, within _____ days of receiving written notice from Lender, Borrower will be in default.

5. **Lender's Rights.** If Borrower is in default, Lender may exercise the remedies contained in the UCC for the state of _____

and any other remedies legally available to Lender. Before exercising such remedies, Lender will provide at least ten days' advance notice, as provided in Paragraph 6. Lender may, for example:

A. remove the Secured Property from the place where it is then located

B. require Borrower to make the Secured Property available to Lender at a place designated by Lender that is reasonably convenient to Borrower and Lender, or

C. sell, lease, or otherwise dispose of the Secured Property.

6. **Notice.** Any notice may be delivered to a party at the address that follows a party's signature below, or to a new address that a party designates in writing. A notice may be delivered:

A. in person

B. by certified mail, or

C. by overnight courier.

7. **Entire Agreement.** This is the entire agreement between the parties. It replaces and supersedes any and all oral agreements between the parties, as well as any prior writings.

8. **Successors and Assigns.** This agreement binds and benefits the parties' heirs, successors, and assigns.

9. **Governing Law.** This agreement will be governed by and construed in accordance with the laws of the state of _____ .

10. **Counterparts.** The parties may sign several identical counterparts of this agreement. Any fully signed counterpart shall be treated as an original.

11. **Modification.** This agreement may be modified only in writing.

12. **Waiver.** If one party waives any term or provision of this agreement at any time, that waiver will be effective only for the specific instance and specific purpose for which the waiver was given. If either party fails to exercise or delays exercising any of its rights or remedies under this agreement, that party retains the right to enforce that term or provision at a later time.

13. **Severability.** If any court determines that any provision of this agreement is invalid or unenforceable, any such invalidity or unenforceability will affect only that provision and will not make any other provision of this agreement invalid or unenforceable and such provision shall be modified, amended, or limited only to the extent necessary to render it valid and enforceable.

_____   _____

Lender's Signature   Date

_____

Print name

_____

Address

_____

Address

_____   _____

Borrower's Signature   Date

_____

Print name

_____

Address

_____

Address

UCC Financing Statement

UCC FINANCING STATEMENT
FOLLOW INSTRUCTIONS (front and back) CAREFULLY

A. NAME & PHONE OF CONTACT AT FILER [optional]

B. SEND ACKNOWLEDGMENT TO: (Name and Address)

THE ABOVE SPACE IS FOR FILING OFFICE USE ONLY

1. DEBTOR'S EXACT FULL LEGAL NAME - insert only one debtor name (1a or 1b) - do not abbreviate or combine names

1a. ORGANIZATION'S NAME			

OR

1b. INDIVIDUAL'S LAST NAME	FIRST NAME	MIDDLE NAME	SUFFIX

1c. MAILING ADDRESS	CITY	STATE	POSTAL CODE	COUNTRY

1d. TAX ID #: SSN OR EIN	ADD'L INFO RE ORGANIZATION DEBTOR	1e. TYPE OF ORGANIZATION	1f. JURISDICTION OF ORGANIZATION	1g. ORGANIZATIONAL ID #, if any	☐ NONE

2. ADDITIONAL DEBTOR'S EXACT FULL LEGAL NAME - insert only one debtor name (2a or 2b) - do not abbreviate or combine names

2a. ORGANIZATION'S NAME			

OR

2b. INDIVIDUAL'S LAST NAME	FIRST NAME	MIDDLE NAME	SUFFIX

2c. MAILING ADDRESS	CITY	STATE	POSTAL CODE	COUNTRY

2d. TAX ID #: SSN OR EIN	ADD'L INFO RE ORGANIZATION DEBTOR	2e. TYPE OF ORGANIZATION	2f. JURISDICTION OF ORGANIZATION	2g. ORGANIZATIONAL ID #, if any	☐ NONE

3. SECURED PARTY'S NAME (or NAME of TOTAL ASSIGNEE of ASSIGNOR S/P) - insert only one secured party name (3a or 3b)

3a. ORGANIZATION'S NAME			

OR

3b. INDIVIDUAL'S LAST NAME	FIRST NAME	MIDDLE NAME	SUFFIX

3c. MAILING ADDRESS	CITY	STATE	POSTAL CODE	COUNTRY

4. This FINANCING STATEMENT covers the following collateral:

5. ALTERNATIVE DESIGNATION [if applicable]:	☐ LESSEE/LESSOR	☐ CONSIGNEE/CONSIGNOR	☐ BAILEE/BAILOR	☐ SELLER/BUYER	☐ AG. LIEN	☐ NON-UCC FILING

6. ☐ This FINANCING STATEMENT is to be filed [for record] (or recorded) in the REAL ESTATE RECORDS Attach Addendum [if applicable]	7. Check to REQUEST SEARCH REPORT(S) on Debtor(s) [ADDITIONAL FEE] [optional]	☐ All Debtors	☐ Debtor 1	☐ Debtor 2

8. OPTIONAL FILER REFERENCE DATA

FILING OFFICE COPY — NATIONAL UCC FINANCING STATEMENT (FORM UCC1) (REV. 07/29/98)

UCC Financing Statement Instructions

Instructions for National UCC Financing Statement (Form UCC1)

Please type or laser-print this form. Be sure it is completely legible. Read all Instructions, especially Instruction 1; correct Debtor name is crucial. Follow Instructions completely.

Fill in form very carefully; mistakes may have important legal consequences. If you have questions, consult your attorney. Filing office cannot give legal advice. Do not insert anything in the open space in the upper portion of this form; it is reserved for filing office use.

When properly completed, send Filing Office Copy, with required fee, to filing office. If you want an acknowledgment, complete item B and, if filing in a filing office that returns an acknowledgment copy furnished by filer, you may also send Acknowledgment Copy; otherwise detach. If you want to make a search request, complete item 7 (after reading Instruction 7 below) and send Search Report Copy, otherwise detach. Always detach Debtor and Secured Party Copies.

If you need to use attachments, use 8-1/2 X 11 inch sheets and put at the top of each sheet the name of the first Debtor, formatted exactly as it appears in item 1 of this form; you are encouraged to use Addendum (Form UCC1Ad).

A. To assist filing offices that might wish to communicate with filer, filer may provide information in item A. This item is optional.

B. Complete item B if you want an acknowledgment sent to you. If filing in a filing office that returns an acknowledgment copy furnished by filer, present simultaneously with this form a carbon or other copy of this form for use as an acknowledgment copy.

1. **Debtor name**: Enter only one Debtor name in item 1, an organization's name (1a) or an individual's name (1b). Enter Debtor's exact full legal name. Don't abbreviate.

1a. Organization Debtor. "Organization" means an entity having a legal identity separate from its owner. A partnership is an organization; a sole proprietorship is not an organization, even if it does business under a trade name. If Debtor is a partnership, enter exact full legal name of partnership; you need not enter names of partners as additional Debtors. If Debtor is a registered organization (e.g., corporation, limited partnership, limited liability company), it is advisable to examine Debtor's current filed charter documents to determine Debtor's correct name, organization type, and jurisdiction of organization.

1b. Individual Debtor. "Individual" means a natural person; this includes a sole proprietorship, whether or not operating under a trade name. Don't use prefixes (Mr., Mrs., Ms.). Use suffix box only for titles of lineage (Jr., Sr., III) and not for other suffixes or titles (e.g., M.D.). Use married woman's personal name (Mary Smith, not Mrs. John Smith). Enter individual Debtor's family name (surname) in Last Name box, first given name in First Name box, and all additional given names in Middle Name box.

For both organization and individual Debtors: Don't use Debtor's trade name, DBA, AKA, FKA, Division name, etc. in place of or combined with Debtor's legal name; you may add such other names as additional Debtors if you wish (but this is neither required nor recommended).

1c. An address is always required for the Debtor named in 1a or 1b.

1d. Debtor's taxpayer identification number (tax ID #) — social security number or employer identification number — may be required in some states.

1e,f,g. "Additional information re organization Debtor" is always required. Type of organization and jurisdiction of organization as well as Debtor's exact legal name can be determined from Debtor's current filed charter document. Organizational ID #, if any, is assigned by the agency where the charter document was filed; this is different from tax ID #; this should be entered preceded by the 2-character U.S. Postal identification of state of organization if one of the United States (e.g., CA12345, for a California corporation whose organizational ID # is 12345); if agency does not assign organizational ID #, check box in item 1g indicating "none."

Note: If Debtor is a trust or a trustee acting with respect to property held in trust, enter Debtor's name in item 1 and attach Addendum (Form UCC1Ad) and check appropriate box in item 17. If Debtor is a decedent's estate, enter name of deceased individual in item 1b and attach Addendum (Form UCC1Ad) and check appropriate box in item 17. If Debtor is a transmitting utility or this Financing Statement is filed in connection with a Manufactured-Home Transaction or a Public-Finance Transaction as defined in applicable Commercial Code, attach Addendum (Form UCC1Ad) and check appropriate box in item 18.

2. If an additional Debtor is included, complete item 2, determined and formatted per Instruction 1. To include further additional Debtors, or one or more additional Secured Parties, attach either Addendum (Form UCC1Ad) or other additional page(s), using correct name format. Follow Instruction 1 for determining and formatting additional names.

3. Enter information for Secured Party or Total Assignee, determined and formatted per Instruction 1. If there is more than one Secured Party, see Instruction 2. If there has been a total assignment of the Secured Party's interest prior to filing this form, you may either (1) enter Assignor S/P's name and address in item 3 and file an Amendment (Form UCC3) [see item 5 of that form]; or (2) enter Total Assignee's name and address in item 3 and, if you wish, also attaching Addendum (Form UCC1Ad) giving Assignor S/P's name and address in item 12.

4. Use item 4 to indicate the collateral covered by this Financing Statement. If space in item 4 is insufficient, put the entire collateral description or continuation of the collateral description on either Addendum (Form UCC1Ad) or other attached additional page(s).

5. If filer desires (at filer's option) to use titles of lessee and lessor, or consignee and consignor, or seller and buyer (in the case of accounts or chattel paper), or bailee and bailor instead of Debtor and Secured Party, check the appropriate box in item 5. If this is an agricultural lien (as defined in applicable Commercial Code) filing or is otherwise not a UCC security interest filing (e.g., a tax lien, judgment lien, etc.), check the appropriate box in item 5, complete items 1-7 as applicable and attach any other items required under other law.

6. If this Financing Statement is filed as a fixture filing or if the collateral consists of timber to be cut or as-extracted collateral, complete items 1-5, check the box in item 6, and complete the required information (items 13, 14 and/or 15) on Addendum (Form UCC1Ad).

7. This item is optional. Check appropriate box in item 7 to request Search Report(s) on all or some of the Debtors named in this Financing Statement. The Report will list all Financing Statements on file against the designated Debtor on the date of the Report, including this Financing Statement. There is an additional fee for each Report. If you have checked a box in item 7, file Search Report Copy together with Filing Officer Copy and Acknowledgment Copy). Note: Not all states do searches and not all states will honor a search request made via this form; some states require a separate request form.

8. This item is optional and is for filer's use only. For filer's convenience of reference, filer may enter in item 8 any identifying information (e.g., Secured Party's loan number, law firm file number, Debtor's name or other identification, state in which form is being filed, etc.) that filer may find useful.

Loan Log

Name of Lender: _____

Name of Borrower: _____

Original Amount Borrowed: $_____

Date Loan Made: _____

Payment number	Payment due date	Total amount due	Payment paid date	Total amount paid	Principal paid	Interest paid	Late payment Date paid	Late fee	Evidence of payment	Other

Gift Letter: Basic

[*borrower name*] _____

[*borrower address*] _____

[*borrower address*] _____

To [*borrower first name*]:

By my signature below, I hereby gift $_____ to you to use as you wish. I expect no repayment or services in return for this gift.

[*signature of giver*] _____

[*printed name of giver*] _____

[*address*] _____

Date: _____

Gift Letter: Loan Repayment Forgiveness

[*borrower name*] _____

[*borrower address*] _____

[*borrower address*] _____

To [*borrower first name*]:

I made a loan of $[*total loan amount*] to you on [*loan date*]. This loan has an upcoming payment due from you to me on [*due date of payment to be forgiven*] in the amount of $_____ ("Loan Payment").

By my signature below, I hereby forgive all of this Loan Payment.

By signing this letter, I understand that I do not waive the right to choose to receive subsequent Loan Payments under the Promissory Note signed by the borrower on [*date note signed*].

[*signature of giver*] _____

[*printed name of giver*] _____

[*address*] _____

Date: _____

Index

Five Cs of credit evaluation, 34–35

Flexibility
  collateral and loan defaults,
    108–109
  lack of, defaults and, 222
  in repayment plans, 11–12, 15,
    20
  restructuring a loan and, 220

Foreclosure. *See* Collateral

Friends-and-family loans. *See*
  Lenders; Private loans

Fundraising. *See* Financing options

G

GEM Study, 2

Gift givers
  business plan requested by, 84
  defined, 5
  overview, 226
  updating on progress, 211–212
  See also Gifts

Gift Letter, 229–232, 268–269

Gifts
  disguised, tax liabilities and,
    54–55
  family control of, 228
  forgiving loans, 230–232, 269
  IRS assuming family group
    transactions to be, 54, 58
  IRS assuming too little interest
    as, 55–56, 182
  IRS limits on gift amounts,
    227–228, 231–232
  IRS rules and loan forgiving,
    230–232

  table comparing features of, 4
  written documentation (gift
    letter), 229–232, 268–269

Grace periods
  in promissory note, 178,
    187–188
  use of, 218–219

Graduated (start-up) loans, 118,
  120–121, 185, 205–206, 251–253

H

Hidden agendas, caution against
  lenders with, 16

Holiday cards, 211

Home, as collateral, 52, 194

Home equity, as financing source,
  28, 29–30

I

Incentives, offering, 160–161

Income statement, 92

Informal investment. *See* Private
  investment

Informal loans. *See* Private loans

ING, interest rates, 115

Intangible assets, 109, 194

Intellectual property, 109, 194

Interest-only loans, 121–122, 126,
  186, 207, 257–259

Interest rates
  adjustable, 116, 160–161
  Applicable Federal Rate (AFR),
    55–56, 112
  arriving at satisfactory range
    of, 116

NOLO *Keep Up to Date*

 Go to **Nolo.com/newsletters/index.html** to sign up for free newsletters and discounts on Nolo products.

- **Nolo Briefs.** Our monthly email newsletter with great deals and free information.

- **Nolo's Special Offer.** A monthly newsletter with the biggest Nolo discounts around.

- **BizBriefs.** Tips and discounts on Nolo products for business owners and managers.

- **Landlord's Quarterly.** Deals and free tips just for landlords and property managers, too.

 Don't forget to check for updates at **Nolo.com.** Under "Products," find this book and click "Legal Updates."

Let Us Hear From You

 Comments on this book? We want to hear 'em. Email us at feedback@nolo.com.

NOLO® *Online Legal Forms*

Nolo offers a large library of legal solutions and forms, created by Nolo's in-house legal staff. These reliable documents can be prepared in minutes.

Online Legal Solutions

- **Incorporation.** Incorporate your business in any state.
- **LLC Formations.** Gain asset protection and pass-through tax status in any state.
- **Wills.** Nolo has helped people make over 2 million wills. Is it time to make or revise yours?
- **Living Trust (avoid probate).** Plan now to save your family the cost, delays, and hassle of probate.
- **Trademark.** Protect the name of your business or product.
- **Provisional Patent.** Preserve your rights under patent law and claim "patent pending" status.

Online Legal Forms

Nolo.com has hundreds of top quality legal forms available for download—bills of sale, promissory notes, nondisclosure agreements, LLC operating agreements, corporate minutes, commercial lease and sublease, motor vehicle bill of sale, consignment agreements and many, many more.

Review Your Documents

Many lawyers in Nolo's consumer-friendly lawyer directory will review Nolo documents for a very reasonable fee. Check their detailed profiles at **www.nolo.com/lawyers/index.html**.

Nolo's Bestselling Books

The Small Business Start-Up Kit
A Step-by-Step Legal Guide
$29.99

Nolo's Quick LLC
All You Need to Know About Limited Liability Companies
$29.99

Tax Savvy for Small Business
$39.99

Deduct It!
Lower Your Small Business Taxes
$34.99

Every Nolo title is available in print and for download at Nolo.com.

NOLO® *Law for All*

Find a Business Attorney

- *Qualified lawyers*
- *In-depth profiles*
- *Respectful service*

When you want help with your small business, you don't want just any lawyer—you want an expert in the field, who can provide up-to-the-minute advice to help you organize and run your enterprise so that you don't fall victim to legal pitfalls. You need a lawyer who has the experience and knowledge to answer your questions about protecting your personal assets, hiring and firing employees, drafting contracts, protecting your name and trademarks and a dozen other common business concerns.

Nolo's Lawyer Directory is unique because it provides an extensive profile of every lawyer. You'll learn about not only each lawyer's education, professional history, legal specialties, credentials and fees, but also about their philosophy of practicing law and how they like to work with clients. It's all crucial information when you're looking for someone to help you avoid as many legal problems as you can and solve the ones you can't.

All lawyers listed in Nolo's directory are in good standing with their state bar association. They all pledge to work diligently and respectfully with clients—communicating regularly, providing a written agreement about how legal matters will be handled, sending clear and detailed bills, and more. And many directory lawyers will review Nolo documents, such as a will or living trust, for a fixed fee, to help you get the advice you need.

WWW.NOLO.COM

The attorneys shown above are fictitious. Any resemblance to an actual attorney is purely coincidental.

3 1901 04873 7284